DEFENDING AI RESEARCH

CSLI
Lecture Notes
No. 49

DEFENDING AI RESEARCH
A Collection of Essays
and Reviews

John McCarthy

CENTER FOR THE STUDY OF
LANGUAGE AND INFORMATION
STANFORD, CALIFORNIA

Library of Congress Cataloging-in-Publication Data

McCarthy, John, 1927–
    Defending AI research : a collection of essays and reviews / John
McCarthy.
        p.   cm. — (CSLI lecture notes ; no. 49)
    Includes bibliographical references (p.).
    ISBN 1-57586-018-X (pbk. : alk. paper). — ISBN 1-57586-019-8
(hardcover : alk. paper)
    1. Artificial intelligence—Research.   I. Title. II. Series.
Q335.7.M33 1996
    006.3—dc20   96-26545
                                                CIP

Chapter 1, "An Unreasonable Book." All references in this chapter refer to *Computer Power and Human Reason*, by Joseph Weizenbaum; San Francisco: W.H. Freeman Co., 1975.

Chapter 2, "Weizenbaum Again—Sermon to Physicists." Reprinted with permission from *Physics Today*, v. 30, no. 1 (January 1977), pp. 68, 70–71. Copyright 1977 American Institute of Physics.

Chapter 3, "Review of 'Artificial Intelligence: A General Survey,'" originally appeared in *Artificial Intelligence*, v. 5, no. 3 (1974), pp. 317–322.

Chapter 8, "Review of the *Emperor's New Mind*," originally appeared in *Bulletin of the American Mathematical Society*, v. 23, no. 2, October 1990, pp. 606–616.

Chapter 10, "Review of *The Question of Artificial Intelligence*," originally appeared in *Annals of the History of Computing*, v. 10, no. 3 (1988), pp. 224–229.

Chapter 11, "Review of *Cognitive Science and Concepts of Mind*," originally appeared in *Quarterly Review of Biology*, v. 67, no. 3 (Sept. 1992), p. 397.

Chapter 13, "Review of *What Computers Still Can't Do*," originally appeared in *Artificial Intelligence*, v. 80, no. 1 (Jan. 1996), pp. 143–150.

Chapter 16, "Review of *Weapons and Hope*," originally appeared in *Reason*, v. 16, no. 7 (Dec. 1984), pp. 53–55.

Chapter 17, "Review of *The Fifth Generation—Artificial Intelligence and Japan's Computer Challenge to the World*," originally appeared in *Reason*, v. 15, no. 12 (April 1984), pp. 53–54.

Contents

Preface

On a number of occasions I have been elected by colleagues and by editors of journals to defend artificial intelligence research from various attacks.

These attacks come from a number of directions.

- Those which claim that artificial intelligence is an incoherent concept philosophically. This is in the ancient tradition of philosophers telling scientists what they must not think about. Hubert Dreyfus, John Searle are examples, and to a lesser extent, so are John Haugeland and James Fetzer. It is often difficult to determine whether these authors are asserting limitations on what behavior computer programs can exhibit or are saying that no matter what it does, it wouldn't count as intelligent.

- Those which claim that artificial intelligence research is immoral, because it is "obscene" and anti-human and moreover caters to the military-industrial complex. Joseph Weizenbaum represents this view here along with some of the articles in the Bloomfield collection. This is the point of view most allied to the general anti-science point of view widespread in the literary culture or to the anti-bourgeois science point of view expressed by Marxists like Kamin, Lewontin and Rose.

- Those which claim artificial intelligence implemented in a computer is impossible for mathematical reasons. Here we have Roger Penrose following a path blazed some years earlier by John Lucas.

- Those which claim that the research is bad and isn't making progress—and maybe can't make progress. Sir James Lighthill is a representative of his view, and Hubert Dreyfus makes similar claims.

vii

With the exception of Fetzer and Haugeland, the above statements have been based on sufficiently general principles as not to require actually reading or referring to research papers in the field.

I will leave specific arguments to the reviews themselves and make a few remarks about motivations for the attacks and their effects. The effects can be described more readily than the motivations so I'll start with them.

The effects have been moderate. No major line of AI research has been abandoned, and I know of no major influence of these attacks on personnel decisions. This is quite different from the situation in studies of human intelligence, where political correctness has intimidated many researchers into abandoning the field. Very likely the attacks have increased the amplitude of funding fluctuations. The Lighthill report had substantial temporary effects in Britain. Attacks from various points of view, both from the left and from the right, have affected social sciences much more than any attacks have affected AI. I emphasize this point, because some of my fellow AI researchers have taken the uninformed criticism harder than I recommend.

The motivations are various. In a few cases, they have been leftist political. Someone who has become leftist for a variety of reasons does his bit for the cause by criticizing AI.

Others are philosophical—an application to AI of ideas from the philosophy of mind that simply don't fit.

There is some criticism of AI from a post-modernist point of view, but mainly we have been spared, and I haven't reviewed anything written from that point of view.

1

An Unreasonable Book

This moralistic and incoherent book uses computer science and technology as an illustration to support the view promoted by Lewis Mumford, Theodore Roszak, and Jacques Ellul, that science has led to an immoral view of man and the world. I am frightened by its arguments that certain research should not be done if it is based on or might result in an "obscene" picture of the world and man. Worse yet, the book's notion of "obscenity" is vague enough to admit arbitrary interpretations by activist bureaucrats.

1.1 It's Hard to Figure Out What He Really Believes...

Weizenbaum's style involves making extreme statements which are later qualified by contradictory statements. Therefore, almost any quotation is out of context, making it difficult to summarize his contentions accurately. The following passages illustrate the difficulty:

> In 1935, Michael Polanyi [British chemist and philosopher of science, was told by] Nicolai Bukharin, one of the leading theoreticians of the Russian Communist party, ... [that] 'under socialism the conception of science pursued for its own sake would disappear, for the interests of scientists would spontaneously turn to the problems of the current Five Year Plan.' Polanyi sensed then that 'the scientific outlook appeared to have produced a mechanical conception of man and history in which there was no place for science itself.' And further that 'this conception denied altogether any intrinsic power to thought

and thus denied any grounds for claiming freedom of thought' (page 1).

Well, that's clear enough; Weizenbaum favors freedom of thought and science and is worried about threats to them. But on page 265, we have

> Scientists who continue to prattle on about 'knowledge for its own sake' in order to exploit that slogan for their self-serving ends have detached science and knowledge from any contact with the real world.

Here Weizenbaum seems to be against pure science, i.e. research motivated solely by curiosity. We also have

> With few exceptions, there have been no results, from over twenty years of artificial intelligence research, that have found their way into industry generally or into the computer industry in particular (page 229).

This again suggests that industrial results are necessary to validate science.

> Science promised man power. But as so often happens when people are seduced by promises of power ... the price actually paid is servitude and impotence.

This is from the book jacket. Presumably the publisher regards it as a good summary of the book's main point.

> I will, in what follows, try to maintain the position that there is nothing wrong with viewing man as an information processor (or indeed as anything else nor with attempting to understand him from that perspective, providing, however, that we never act as though any single perspective can comprehend the whole man (page 140).

We can certainly live with that, but

> Not only has our unbounded feeding on science caused us to become dependent on it, but, as happens with many other drugs taken in increasing dosages, science has been gradually converted into a slow acting poison (page 13).

These are qualified by

> I argue for the rational use of science and technology, not for its mystification, let alone its abandonment (page 256).

In reference to the proposal for a moratorium on certain experiments with recombinant DNA because they might be dangerous, we have

> Theirs is certainly a step in the right direction, and their initiative is to be applauded. Still, one may ask, why do they feel they have to give a reason for what they recommend at all? Is not the overriding obligation on men, including men of science, to exempt life itself from the madness of treating everything as an object, a sufficient reason, and one that does not even have to be spoken? Why does it have to be explained? It would appear that even the noblest acts of the most well-meaning people are poisoned by the corrosive climate of values of our time.

Is Weizenbaum against all experimental biology or even all experiments with DNA? I would hesitate to conclude so from this quote; he may say the direct opposite somewhere else. Weizenbaum's goal of getting lines of research abandoned without even having to give a reason seems unlikely to be achieved except in an atmosphere that combines public hysteria and bureaucratic power. This has happened under conditions of religious enthusiasm and in Nazi Germany, in Stalinist Russia and in the China of the "Cultural Revolution". Most likely it won't happen in America.

> Those who know who and what they are do not need to ask what they should do (page 273).

Let me assure the reader that there is nothing in the book that offers any way to interpret this pomposity. I take it as another plea to be free of the bondage of having to give reasons for his denunciations.

The menace of such grandiloquent precepts is that they require a priesthood to apply them to particular cases, and would-be priests quickly crystallize around any potential center of power. A corollary of this is that people can be attacked for what they are rather than for anything specific they have done. The April 1976 issue of *Ms.* has a poignant illustration of this in an article about "trashing".

> An individual is dehumanized whenever he is treated as less than a whole person (page 266).

This is also subject to priestly interpretation as in the encounter group movement.

> The first kind [of computer application] I would call simply obscene. These are ones whose very contemplation ought to give rise to feelings of disgust in every civilized person. The proposal I have mentioned, that an animal's visual system and brain be coupled to computers, is an example. It represents an attack on life itself. One must wonder what must have happened to the proposers' perception of life, hence to their perceptions of themselves as part of the continuum of life, that they can even think of such a thing, let alone advocated it.

No argument is offered that might be answered, and no attempt is made to define criteria of acceptability. I think Weizenbaum and the scientists who have praised the book may be surprised at some of the repressive uses to which the book will be put. However, they will be able to point to passages in the book with quite contrary sentiments, so the repression won't be their fault.

1.2   But Here's a Try at Summarizing

As these inconsistent passages show, it isn't easy to determine Weizenbaum's position, but the following seem to be the book's main points:

1. Weizenbaum doesn't name any specific task that computers cannot carry out, because he wishes

> ... to avoid the unnecessary, interminable, and ultimately sterile exercise of making a catalogue of what computers will and will not be able to do, either here and now or ever.

It is also stated that human and machine reasoning are incomparable and that the sensory experience of a human is essential for human reasoning.

2. There are tasks that computers should not be programmed to do. Some are tasks Weizenbaum thinks shouldn't be done at all—perhaps for political reasons. One may quarrel with his politics, and I do, but obviously computers shouldn't do what shouldn't be done. However, Weizenbaum also objects to computer hookups to animal brains and

computer conducted psychiatric interviews. As to the former, I couldn't tell whether he is an anti-vivisectionist, but he seems to have additional reasons for calling them "obscene". The objection to computers doing psychiatric interviews also has a component beyond the conviction that they would necessarily do it badly. Thus he says,

> What can the psychiatrist's image of his patient be when he sees himself, as a therapist, not as an engaged human being acting as a healer, but as an information processor following rules, etc.?

This seems like the renaissance era religious objections to dissecting the human body that came up when science revived. Even the Popes eventually convinced themselves that regarding the body as a machine for scientific or medical purposes was quite compatible with regarding it as the temple of the soul. Recently they have taken the same view of studying mental mechanisms for scientific or psychiatric purposes.

3. Science has led people to a wrong view of the world and of life. The view is characterized as mechanistic, and the example of clockwork is given. (It seems strange for a computer scientist to give this example, because the advance of the computer model over older mechanistic models is that computers can and clockwork can't make decisions.) Apparently analysis of a living system as composed of interacting parts rather than treating it as an unanalyzed whole is bad.

4. Science is not the sole or even main source of reliable general knowledge. However, he doesn't propose any other sources of knowledge or say what the limits of scientific knowledge is except to characterize certain thoughts as "obscene".

5. Certain people and institutions are attacked. These include the Department of "Defense" (sic), *Psychology Today*, *The New York Times* Data Bank, compulsive computer programmers, Kenneth Colby, Marvin Minsky, Roger Schank, Allen Newell, Herbert Simon, J.W. Forrester, Edward Fredkin, B.F. Skinner, Warren McCulloch (until he was old), Laplace and Leibniz.

6. Certain political and social views are taken for granted. The view that U.S. policy in Vietnam was "murderous" is used to support an attack on "logicality" (as opposed to "rationality") and the view of science as a

"slow acting poison". The phrase "It may be that the people's cultivated and finally addictive hunger for private automobiles . . ." (page 30) makes psychological, sociological, political, and technological presumptions all in one phrase. Similarly, "Men could instead choose to have truly safe automobiles, decent television, decent housing for everyone, or comfortable, safe, and widely distributed mass transportation." presumes wide agreement about what these things are, what is technologically feasible, what the effects of changed policies would be, and what activities aimed at changing people's taste are permissible for governments.

1.3   The ELIZA Example

Perhaps the most interesting part of the book is the account of his own program ELIZA that parodies Rogerian non-directive psychotherapy and his anecdotal account of how some people ascribe intelligence and personality to it. In my opinion, it is quite natural for people who don't understand the notion of algorithm to imagine that a computer computes analogously to the way a human reasons. This leads to the idea that accurate computation entails correct reasoning and even to the idea that computer malfunctions are analogous to human neuroses and psychoses. Actually, programming a computer to draw interesting conclusions from premises is very difficult and only limited success has been attained. However, the effect of these natural misconceptions shouldn't be exaggerated; people readily understand the truth when it is explained, especially when it applies to a matter that concerns them. In particular, when an executive excuses a mistake by saying that he placed excessive faith in a computer, a certain skepticism is called for.

Colby's (1973) study is interesting in this connection, but the interpretation below is mine. Colby had psychiatrists interview patients over a teletype line and also had them interview his PARRY program that simulates a paranoid. Other psychiatrists were asked to decide from the transcripts whether the interview was with a man or with a program, and they did no better than chance. However, since PARRY is incapable of the simplest causal reasoning, if you ask, "How do you know the people following you are Mafia" and get a reply that they look like Italians, this must be a man not PARRY. Curiously, it is easier to imitate (well enough to fool a psychiatrist) the emotional side of a man than his intellectual side. Probably the subjects expected the machine to have more logical ability, and this expectation contributed to their mistakes. Alas, random selection from the directory of the Association for Computing Machinery did no better.

It seems to me that ELIZA and PARRY show only that people, including psychiatrists, often have to draw conclusions on slight evidence, and are therefore easily fooled. If I am right, two sentences of instruction would allow them to do better.

In his 1966 paper on ELIZA (cited as 1965), Weizenbaum writes,

One goal for an augmented ELIZA program is thus a system which already has access to a store of information about some aspect of the real world and which, by means of conversational interaction with people, can reveal both what it knows, i.e. behave as an information retrieval system, and where its knowledge ends and needs to be augmented. Hopefully the augmentation of its knowledge will also be a direct consequence of its conversational experience. It is precisely the prospect that such a program will converse with many people and learn something from each of them which leads to the hope that it will prove an interesting and even useful conversational partner.

Too bad he didn't successfully pursue this goal; no one else has. I think success would have required a better understanding of formalization than is exhibited in the book.

1.4   What Does He Say About Computers?

While Weizenbaum's main conclusions concern science in general and are moralistic in character, some of his remarks about computer science and AI are worthy of comment.

1. He concludes that since a computer cannot have the experience of a man, it cannot understand a man. There are three points to be made in reply. First, humans share each other's experiences and those of machines or animals only to a limited extent. In particular, men and women have different experiences. Nevertheless, it is common in literature for a good writer to show greater understanding of the experience of the

opposite sex than a poorer writer of that sex. Second, the notion of experience is poorly understood; if we understood it better, we could reason about whether a machine could have a simulated or vicarious experience normally confined to humans. Third, what we mean by understanding is poorly understood, so we don't yet know how to define whether a machine understands something or not.

2. Like his predecessor critics of artificial intelligence, Taube, Dreyfus and Lighthill, Weizenbaum is impatient, implying that if the problem hasn't been solved in twenty years, it is time to give up. Genetics took about a century to go from Mendel to the genetic code for proteins, and still has a long way to go before we will fully understand the genetics and evolution of intelligence and behavior. Artificial intelligence may be just as difficult. My current answer to the question of when machines will reach human-level intelligence is that a precise calculation shows that we are between 1.7 and 3.1 Einsteins and .3 Manhattan Projects away from the goal. However, the current research is producing the information on which the Einstein will base himself and is producing useful capabilities all the time.

3. The book confuses computer simulation of a phenomenon with its formalization in logic. A simulation is only one kind of formalization and not often the most useful—even to a computer. In the first place, logical and mathematical formalizations can use partial information about a system insufficient for a simulation. Thus the law of conservation of energy tells us much about possible energy conversion systems before we define even one of them. Even when a simulation program is available, other formalizations are necessary even to make good use of the simulation. This review isn't the place for a full explanation of the relations between these concepts.

Like *Punch*'s famous curate's egg, the book is good in parts. Thus it raises the following interesting issues:

1. What would it mean for a computer to hope or be desperate for love? Answers to these questions depend on being able to formalize (not simulate) the phenomena in question. My guess is that adding a notion of hope to an axiomatization of belief and wanting might not be difficult.

The study of *propositional attitudes* in philosophical logic points in that direction.

2. Do differences in experience make human and machine intelligence necessarily so different that it is meaningless to ask whether a machine can be more intelligent than a machine? My opinion is that comparison will turn out to be meaningful. After all, most people have not doubt that humans are more intelligent than turkeys. Weizenbaum's examples of the dependence of human intelligence on sensory abilities seem even refutable, because we recognize no fundamental difference in humanness in people who are severely handicapped sensorily, e.g. the deaf, dumb and blind or paraplegics.

1.5 In Defense of the Unjustly Attacked—Some of whom are Innocent

Here are defenses of Weizenbaum's targets. They are not guaranteed to entirely suit the defendees.

Weizenbaum's conjecture that the Defense Department supports speech recognition research in order to be able to snoop on telephone conversations is biased, baseless, false, and seems motivated by political malice. The committee of scientists that proposed the project advanced quite different considerations, and the high officials who made the final decisions are not ogres. Anyway their other responsibilities leave them no time for complicated and devious considerations. I put this one first, because I think the failure of many scientists to defend the Defense Department against attacks they know are unjustified, is unjust in itself, and furthermore has harmed the country.

Weizenbaum doubts that computer speech recognition will have cost-effective applications beyond snooping on phone conversations. He also says, "There is no question in my mind that there is no pressing human problem that will be more easily solved because such machines exist." I worry more about whether the programs can be made to work before the sponsor loses patience. Once they work, costs will come down. Winograd pointed out to me that many possible household applications of computers may not be feasible without some computer speech recognition. One needs to think *both* about how to solve recognized problems and about opportunities to put new technological possibilities to good use. The telephone was not invented by a committee considering already identified problems of communication.

Referring to *Psychology Today* as a cafeteria simply excites the snobbery of those who would like to consider their psychological knowledge to be above the popular level. So far as I know, professional and academic psychologists welcome the opportunity offered by *Psychology Today* to explain their ideas to a wide public. They might even buy a cut-down version of Weizenbaum's book if he asks them nicely. Hmm, they might even buy this review.

Weizenbaum has invented a *New York Times Data Bank* different from the one operated by *The New York Times*—and possibly better. The real one stores abstracts written by humans and doesn't use the tapes intended for typesetting machines. As a result the user has access only to abstracts and cannot search on features of the stories themselves, i.e. he is at the mercy of what the abstractors thought was important at the time.

Using computer programs as psychotherapists, as Colby proposed, would be moral if it would cure people. Unfortunately, computer science isn't up to it, and maybe the psychiatrists aren't either.

I agree with Minsky in criticizing the reluctance of art theorists to develop formal theories. George Birkhoff's formal theory was probably wrong, but he shouldn't have been criticized for trying. The problem seems very difficult to me, and I have made no significant progress in responding to a challenge from Arthur Koestler to tell how a computer program might make or even recognize jokes. Perhaps some reader of this review might have more success.

There is a whole chapter attacking "compulsive computer programmers" or "hackers". This mythical beast lives in the computer laboratory, is an expert on all the ins and outs of the time-sharing system, elaborates the time-sharing system with arcane features that he never documents, and is always changing the system before he even fixes the bugs in the previous version. All these vices exist, but I can't think of any individual who combines them, and people generally outgrow them. As a laboratory director, I have to protect the interests of people who program only part time against tendencies to over-complicate the facilities. People who spend all their time programming and who exchange information by word of mouth sometimes have to be pressed to make proper writeups. The other side of the issue is that we professors of computer science sometimes lose our ability to write actual computer programs through lack of practice and envy younger people who can spend full time in the laboratory. The phenomenon is well known in other sciences and in other human activities.

Weizenbaum attacks the Yale computer linguist, Roger Schank, as follows—the inner quotes are from Schank:

> What is contributed when it is asserted that 'there exists a conceptual base that is interlingual, onto which linguistic structures in a given language map during the understanding process and out of which such structures are created during generation [of linguistic utterances]'? Nothing at all. For the term 'conceptual base' could perfectly well be replaced by the word 'something'. And who could argue with that so-transformed statement?"

Weizenbaum goes on to say that the real scientific problem "remains as untouched as ever". On the next page he says that unless the "Schank-like scheme" understood the sentence "Will you come to dinner with me this evening?" to mean "a shy young man's desperate longing for love", then the sense in which the system "understands" is "about as weak as the sense in which ELIZA "understood". This good example raises interesting issues and seems to call for some distinctions. Full understanding of the sentence indeed results in knowing about the young man's desire for love, but it would seem that there is a useful lesser level of understanding in which the machine would know only that he would like her to come to dinner.

Contrast Weizenbaum's demanding, more-human-than-thou attitude to Schank and Winograd with his respectful and even obsequious attitude to Chomsky. We have

> The linguist's first task is therefore to write grammars, that is, sets of rules, of particular languages, grammars capable of characterizing all and only the grammatically admissible sentences of those languages, and then to postulate principles from which crucial features of all

such grammars can be deduced. That set of principles would then constitute a universal grammar. Chomsky's hypothesis is, to put it another way, that the rules of such a universal grammar would constitute a kind of projective description of important aspects of the human mind.

There is nothing here demanding that the universal grammar take into account the young man's desire for love. As far as I can see, Chomsky is just as much a rationalist as we artificial intelligentsia.

Chomsky's goal of a universal grammar and Schank's goal of a conceptual base are similar, except that Schank's ideas are further developed, and the performance of his students' programs can be compared with reality. I think they will require drastic revision and may not be on the right track at all, but then I am pursuing a rather different line of research concerning how to represent the basic facts that an intelligent being must know about the world. My idea is to start from epistemology rather than from language, regarding their linguistic representation as secondary. This approach has proved difficult, has attracted few practitioners, and has led to few computer programs, but I still think it's right.

Weizenbaum approves of the Chomsky school's haughty attitude towards Schank, Winograd and other AI based language researchers. On page 184, he states,

> ... many linguists, for example, Noam Chomsky, believe that enough thinking about language remains to be done to occupy them usefully for yet a little while, and that any effort to convert their present theories into computer models would, if attempted by the people best qualified, be a diversion from the main task. And they rightly see no point to spending any of their energies studying the work of the hackers.

This brings the chapter on "compulsive computer programmers" alias "hackers" into a sharper focus. Chomsky's latest book *Reflections on Language* makes no reference to the work of Winograd, Schank, Charniak, Wilks, Bobrow or William Woods to name only a few of those who have developed large computer systems that work with natural language and who write papers on the semantics of natural language. The actual young computer programmers who call themselves hackers and who come closest to meeting Weizenbaum's description don't write papers on natural language. So it seems that the hackers whose work need not be studied are Winograd, Schank, et al. who are professors and senior scientists. The Chomsky school may be embarassed by the fact that it has only recently arrived at the conclusion that the semantics of natural language is more fundamental than its syntax, while AI based researchers have been pursuing this line for fifteen years.

The outside observer should be aware that to some extent this is a pillow fight within M.I.T. Chomsky and Halle are not to be dislodged from M.I.T. and neither is Minsky—whose students have pioneered the AI approach to natural language. Schank is quite secure at Yale. Weizenbaum also has tenure. However, some assistant professorships in linguistics may be at stake, especially at M.I.T.

Allen Newell and Herbert Simon are criticized for being overoptimistic and are considered morally defective for attempting to describe humans as difference-reducing machines. Simon's view that the human is a simple system in a complex environment is singled out for attack. In my opinion, they were overoptimistic, because their GPS model on which they put their bets wasn't good enough. Maybe Newell's current *production system models* will work out better. As to whether human mental structure will eventually turn out to be simple, I vacillate but incline to the view that it will turn out to be one of the most complex biological phenomena.

I regard Forrester's models as incapable of taking into account qualitative changes, and the world models they have built as defective even in their own terms, because they leave out saturation-of-demand effects that cannot be discovered by curve-fitting as long as a sytem is rate-of-expansion limited. Moreover, I don't accept his claim that his models are better suited than the unaided mind in "interpreting how social systems behave", but Weizenbaum's sarcasm on page 246 is unconvincing. He quotes Forrester,

[desirable modes of behavior of the social system] seem to be possible only if we have a good understanding of the system dynamics and are willing to endure the self-discipline and pressures that must accompany the desirable mode.

Weizenbaum comments,

> There is undoubtedly some interpretation of the words 'system' and 'dynamics' which would lend a benign meaning to this observation.

Sorry, but it looks ok to me provided one is suitably critical of Forrester's proposed social goals and the possibility of making the necessary assumptions and putting them into his models.

Skinner's behaviorism that refuses to assign reality to people's internal state seems wrong to me, but we can't call him immoral for trying to convince us of what he thinks is true.

Weizenbaum quotes Edward Fredkin, former director of Project MAC, and the late Warren McCulloch of M.I.T. without giving their names. pp. 241 and 240. Perhaps he thinks a few puzzles will make the book more interesting, and this is so. Fredkin's plea for research in automatic programming seems to overestimate the extent to which our society currently relies on computers for decisions. It also overestimates the ability of the faculty of a particular university to control the uses to which technology will be put, and it underestimates the difficulty of making knowledge based systems of practical use. Weizenbaum is correct in pointing out that Fredkin doesn't mention the existence of genuine conflicts in society, but only the new left sloganeering elsewhere in the book gives a hint as to what he thinks they are and how he proposes to resolve them.

As for the quotation from McCulloch 1956, Minsky tells me "this is a brave attempt to find a dignified sense of freedom within the psychological determinism morass." Probably this can be done better now, but Weizenbaum wrongly implies that McCulloch's 1956 effort is to his moral discredit.

Finally, Weizenbaum attributes to me two statements—both from oral presentations—which I cannot verify. One of them is

> The only reason we have not yet succeeded in simulating every aspect of the real world is that we have been lacking a sufficiently powerful logical calculus. I am working on that problem.

This statement doesn't express my present opinion or my opinion in 1973 when I am alleged to have expressed it in a debate, and no one has been able to find it in the video-tape of the debate.

We can't simulate "every aspect of the real world" because the initial state information is never available, the laws of motion are imperfectly known, and the calculations for a simulation are too extensive. Moreover, simulation wouldn't necessarily answer our questions. Instead, we must find out how to represent in the memory of a computer the information about the real world that is actually available to a machine or organism with given sensory capability, and also how to represent a means of drawing those useful conclusions about the effects of courses of action that can be correctly inferred from the attainable information. Having *a sufficiently powerful logical calculus* is an important part of this problem—but one of the easier parts.

This statement has been quoted in a large fraction of the reviews of Weizenbaum's book (e.g. in *Datamation* and *Nature*) arrogance of the "artificial intelligentsia". Weizenbaum firmly insisted that he heard it in the Lighthill debate and cited his notes as corroboration, but later admitted after reviewing the tape that he didn't, but claimed I must have said it in some other debate. I am confident I didn't say it, because it contradicts views I have held and repeatedly stated since 1959. My present conjecture is that Weizenbaum heard me say something on the importance of formalization, couldn't quite remember what, and quoted "what McCarthy must have said" based on his own misunderstanding of the relation between computer modeling and formalization. (His two chapters on computers show no awareness of the difference between declarative and procedural knowledge or of the discussions in the AI literature of their respective roles). Needless to say, the repeated citation by reviewers of a pompous statement that I never made and which is in opposition to the view that I think represents my major contribution to AI is very offensive.

The second quotation from me is the rhetorical question, *"What do judges know that we cannot tell a computer"*. I'll stand on that if we make it "eventually tell" and especially if we require that it be something that one human can reliably teach another.

1.6 A Summary of Polemical Sins

The speculative sections of the book contain numerous dubious little
theories, such as this one about the dehumanizing effect of of the invention
of the clock:

> The clock had created literally a new reality; and that is what I meant
> when I said earlier that the trick man turned that prepared the scene for
> the rise of modern science was nothing less than the transformation
> of nature and of his perception of reality. It is important to realize that
> this newly created reality was and remains an impoverished version
> of the older one, for it rests on a rejection of those direct experiences
> that formed the basis for, and indeed constituted the old reality. The
> feeling of hunger was rejected as a stimulus for eating; instead one
> ate when an abstract model had achieved a certain state, i.e. when
> the hand of a clock pointed to certain marks on the clock's face (the
> anthropomorphism here is highly significant too), and similarly for
> signals for sleep and rising, and so on.

This idealization of primitive life is simply thoughtless. Like modern
man, primitive man ate when the food was ready, and primitive man
probably had to start preparing it even further in advance. Like modern
man, primitive man lived in families whose members are no more likely
to become hungry all at once than are the members of a present family.

I get the feeling that in toppling this microtheory I am not playing the
game; the theory is intended only to provide an atmosphere, and like the
reader of a novel, I am supposed to suspend disbelief. But the contention
that science has driven us from a psychological Garden of Eden depends
heavily on such word pictures.

By the way, I recall from my last sabbatical at M.I.T. that the *feeling
of hunger* is more often *the direct social stimulus for eating* for the
"hackers" deplored in Chapter 4 than it could have been for primitive
man. Often on a crisp New England night, even as the clock strikes
three, I hear them call to one another, messages flash on the screens, a
flock of hackers magically gathers, and the whole picturesque assembly
rushes chattering off to Chinatown.

I find the book substandard as a piece of polemical writing in the following respects:

1. The author has failed to work out his own positions on the issues he discusses. Making an extreme statement in one place and a contradictory statement in another is no substitute for trying to take all the factors into account and reach a considered position. Unsuspicious readers can come away with a great variety of views, and the book can be used to support contradictory positions.

2. The computer linguists—Winograd, Schank, et al.—are denigrated as hackers and compulsive computer programmers by innuendo.

3. One would like to know more precisely what biological and psychological experiments and computer applications he finds acceptable. Reviewers have already drawn a variety of conclusions on this point.

4. The terms "authentic", "obscene", and "dehumanization" are used as clubs. This is what mathematicians call "proof by intimidation".

5. The book encourages a snobbery that has no need to argue for its point of view but merely utters code words, on hearing which the audience is supposed applaud or hiss as the case may be. The *New Scientist* reviewer certainly salivates in most of the intended places.

6. Finally, when moralizing is both vehement and vague, it invites authoritarian abuse either by existing authority or by new political movements. Imagine, if you can, that this book were the bible of some bureaucracy, e.g. an Office of Technology Assessment, that acquired power over the computing or scientific activities of a university, state, or country. Suppose Weizenbaum's slogans were combined with *the bureaucratic ethic* that holds that any problem can be solved by a law forbidding something and a bureaucracy of eager young lawyers to enforce it. Postulate further a vague *Humane Research Act* and a "public interest" organization with more eager young lawyers suing to get judges to legislate new interpretations of the Act. One can see a laboratory needing more lawyers than scientists and a Humane Research Administrator capable of forbidding or requiring almost anything.

I see no evidence that Weizenbaum forsees his work being used in this way; he doesn't use the phrase *laissez innover* which is the would-be science bureaucrat's analogue of the economist's *laissez faire*, and he never uses the indefinite phrase "it should be decided" which is a common expression of the bureaucratic ethic. However, he has certainly given his fellow computer scientists at least some reason to worry about potential tyranny.

Let me conclude this section with a quotation from Andrew D. White, the first president of Cornell University, that seems applicable to the present situation—not only in computer science, but also in biology.

> In all modern history, interference with science in the supposed interest of religion, no matter how conscientious such interference may have been, has resulted in the direst evils both to religion and to science, and invariably; and, on the other hand, all untrammelled scientific investigation, no matter how dangerous to religion some of its stages my have seemed for the time to be, has invariably resulted in the highest good both of religion and of science.

Substitute *morality* for *religion* and the parallel is clear. Frankly, the feebleness of the reaction to attacks on scientific freedom worries me more than the strength of the attacks.

1.7   What Worries about Computers are Warranted?

Grumbling about Weizenbaum's mistakes and moralizing is not enough. Genuine worries prompted the book, and many people share them. Here are the genuine concerns that I can identify and the opinions of one computer scientist about their resolution: What is the danger that the computer will lead to a false model of man? What is the danger that computers will be misused? Can human-level artificial intelligence be achieved? What, if any, motivational characteristics will it have? Would the achievement of artificial intelligence be good or bad for humanity?

1. Does the computer model lead to a false model of man? Historically, the mechanistic model of the life and the world followed animistic models in accordance with which, priests and medicine men tried to correct malfunctions of the environment and man by inducing spirits to behave better. Replacing them by mechanistic models replaced shamanism by medicine. Roszak explicitly would like to bring these models back, because he finds them more "human", but he ignores the sad fact

that they don't work, because the world isn't constructed that way. The pre-computer mechanistic models of the mind were, in my opinion, unsuccessful, but I think the psychologists pursuing computational models of mental processes may eventually develop a really beneficial psychiatry.

Philosophical and moral thinking hasn't yet found a model of man that relates human beliefs and purposes to the physical world in a plausible way. Some of the unsuccessful attempts have been more mechanistic than others. Both mechanistic and non-mechanistic models have led to great harm when made the basis of political ideology, because they have allowed tortuous reasoning to justify actions that simple human intuition regards as immoral. In my opinion, the relation between beliefs, purposes and wants to the physical world is a complicated but ultimately solvable problem. Computer models can help solve it, and can provide criteria that will enable us to reject false solutions. The latter is more important for now, and computer models are already hastening the decay of dialectical materialism in the Soviet Union.

2. What is the danger that computers will be misused? Up to now, computers have been just another labor-saving technology. I don't agree with Weizenbaum's acceptance of the claim that our society would have been inundated by paper work without computers. Without computers, people would work a little harder and get a little less for their work. However, when home terminals become available, social changes of the magnitude of those produced by the telephone and automobile will occur. I have discussed them elsewhere, and I think they will be good—as were the changes produced by the automobile and the telephone. Tyranny comes from control of the police coupled with a tyrannical ideology; data banks will be a minor convenience. No dictatorship yet has been overthrown for lack of a data bank.

One's estimate of whether technology will work out well in the future is correlated with one's view of how it worked out in the past. I think it has worked out well—e.g. cars were not a mistake—and am optimistic about the future. I feel that much current ideology is a combination of older anti-scientific and anti-technological views with new developments in the political technology of instigating and manipulating fears and guilt feelings.

3. What motivations will artificial intelligence have? It will have what motivations we choose to give it. Those who finally create it should start by motivating it only to answer questions and should have the sense to ask for full pictures of the consequences of alternate actions rather than simply how to achieve a fixed goal, ignoring possible side-effects. Giving it human motivational structure with its shifting goals sensitive to physical state would require a deliberate effort beyond that required to make it behave intelligently.

4. Will artificial intelligence be good or bad? Here we are talking about machines with the same range of intellectual abilities as are posessed by humans. However, the science fiction vision of robots with almost precisely the ability of a human is quite unlikely, because the next generation of computers or even hooking computers together would produce an intelligence that might be qualitatively like that of a human, but thousands of times faster. What would it be like to be able to put a hundred years thought into every decision? I think it is impossible to say whether qualitatively better answers would be obtained; we will have to try it and see.

The achievement of above-human-level artificial intelligence will open to humanity an incredible variety of options. We cannot now fully envisage what these options will be, but it seems apparent that one of the first uses of high-level artificial intelligence will be to determine the consequences of alternate policies governing its use. I think the most likely variant is that man will use artificial intelligence to transform himself, but once its properties and the conequences of its use are known, we may decide not to use it. Science would then be a sport like mountain climbing; the point would be to discover the facts about the world using some stylized limited means. I wouldn't like that, but once man is confronted by the actuality of full AI, they may find our opinion as relevant to them as we would find the opinion of *Pithecanthropus* about whether subsequent evolution took the right course.

5. What shouldn't computers be programmed to do? Obviously one shouldn't program computers to do things that should not be done. Moreover, we shouldn't use programs to mislead ourselves or other people. Apart from that, I find none of Weizenbaum's examples convincing.

However, I doubt the advisability of making robots with human-like motivational and emotional structures that might have rights and duties independently of humans. Moreover, I think it might be dangerous to make a machine that evolved intelligence by responding to a program of rewards and punishments unless its trainers understand the intellectual and motivational structure being evolved.

All these questions merit and have received more extensive discussion, but I think the only rational policy now is to expect the people confronted by the problem to understand their best interests better than we now can. Even if full AI were to arrive next year, this would be right. Correct decisions will require an intense effort that cannot be mobilized to consider an eventuality that is still remote. Imagine asking the presidential candidates to debate on TV what each of them would do about each of the forms that full AI might take.

References:

McCulloch, W.S. (1956) Toward some circuitry of ethical robots or an observational science of the genesis of social evaluation in the mind-like behavior of artifacts. *Acta Biotheoretica*, XI, parts 3/4, 147–156.

2

Weizenbaum Again—Sermon to Physicists

The idea of a stored program computer leads immediately to studying mental processes as abstract computer programs. Artificial intelligence treats problem solving mechanisms non-biologically, and modern cognitive psychology makes information-processing models of the human mind. Both studies have proved fruitful though difficult and have been pursued with ever increasing vigor.

Progress in either study, like Darwinism and like most progress in medicine and biology, moves the scientific picture of man's nature directly away from the subjectivity preferred by modern literary culture. Full success, like successful genetic engineering, will present individuals and society with a bewildering collection of options. Weizenbaum fears both the options he can imagine and the rationalist world-view that computer-modeling reinforces.

He criticizes all present work in artificial intelligence, information-processing-based psychology and computer linguistics as mere technique. In particular he regards the computer linguists as "hackers" whose work there is no point in studying, but he explicitly puts no limit on the potential problem-solving capability of computers except when understanding humans is required. His point is moral, and his arguments use the 1960s technology of moralistic invective.

He finds it immoral for a scientist to adopt certain hypotheses even tentatively, to perform certain experiments or propose certain applications—not because they are dangerous or won't work, but be-

23

cause they are "obscene". He distinguishes between not closing one's mind to a hypothesis (OK) and tentatively adopting it (possibly immoral). Also information processing models of man are OK in principle provided one recognizes that they can't model any "authentically human concern", but no work meeting his criteria is mentioned.

The objectionable hypotheses, experiments and applications include the theory that man is a simple organism in a complex environment, the idea that all reality can be formalized, the idea that what a judge knows can be told to a computer, some experiments with recombinant DNA, connecting animal brains to computers, psychological testing, and using a computer program for psychiatry. Here are some of the arguments:

On psychiatry—"What can the psychiatrist's image of his patient be when he sees himself, as a therapist, not as an engaged human being acting as a healer, but as an information processor following rules, etc.?"

On connecting computers to animal brains—"The first kind [of application] I would call simply obscene. These are ones whose very contemplation ought to give rise to feelings of disgust in every civilized person.'

On a proposed moratorium on some DNA experiments—"why do they feel they have to give a reason for what they recommend at all? Is not the overriding obligation on men, including men of science, to exempt life itself from the madness of treating everything as an object, a sufficient reason, and one that does not even have to be spoken?"

On science in general and pure science in particular—"Not only has our unbounded feeding on science caused us to become dependent on it, but, as happens with many other drugs taken in increasing doses, science has been gradually converted into a slow acting poison." and, "Scientists who continue to prattle on about 'knowledge for its own sake' in order to exploit that slogan for their self-serving ends have detached science and knowledge from any contact with the real world."

A moral principle—"Those who know who and what they are do not need to ask what they should do."

Success in modeling the mind will raise policy issues with both moral and factual aspects. However, the public entitled to decide them has more immediate concerns; imagine asking the 1976 presidential candidates to debate whether computer programs should do psychiatry while there are none that can. When they become concrete, they must be discussed in terms of costs and benefits and not in terms of "obscenity".

As in Darwin's time, science—especially genetics, psychology, sociology and (now) computer science—is being morally pressed to fit its theories to "religion". Many have given in; few will speak out for studying the genetics of human behavior, computer scientists in unrelated fields claimed to have proved that the ABM couldn't work, and physicists claim to show that nuclear explosions can have no peaceful use. When scientists forget their duty to pursue truth wherever the search leads, when they start selecting facts to support comforting world-views or the policies of the good guys, they lose much of their value to society.

3

Review of "Artificial Intelligence: A General Survey"

Professor Lighthill of Cambridge University is a famous hydrodynam-icist with a recent interest in applications to biology. His review of artificial intelligence was at the request of Brian Flowers, then head of the Science Research Council of Great Britain, the main funding body for British university scientific research. Its purpose was to help the Science Research Council decide requests for support of work in AI. Lighthill claims no previous acquaintance with the field, but refers to a large number of authors whose works he consulted, though not to any specific papers.

The *Lighthill Report* is organized around a classification of AI re-search into three categories:

Category A is *advanced automation* or *applications*, and he approves of it in principle. Included in A are some activities that are obviously applied but also activities like computer chess playing that are often done not for themselves but in order to study the structure of intelligent behavior.

Category C comprises studies of the *central nervous system* including computer modeling in support of both neurophysiology and psychology.

Category B is defined as "building robots" and "bridge" between the other two categories. Lighthill defines a robot as a program or device built neither to serve a useful purpose nor to study the central nervous system, which obviously would exclude Unimates, etc. which are generally referred to as industrial robots. Emphasizing the bridge aspect of the definition, Lighthill states as obvious that work in category B is worthwhile only in so far as it contributes to the other categories.

If we take this categorization seriously, then most AI researchers lose intellectual contact with Lighthill immediately, because his three categories have no place for what is or should be our main scientific activity—*studying the structure of information and the structure of problem solving processes independently of applications and independently of its realization in animals or humans.* This study is based on the following ideas:

1. Intellectual activity takes place in a world that has a certain physical and intellectual structure: Physical objects exist, move about, are created and destroyed. Actions that may be performed have effects that are partially known. Entities with goals have available to them certain information about this world. Some of this information may be built in, and some arises from observation, from communication, from reasoning, and by more or less complex processes of retrieval from information bases. Much of this structure is common to the intellectual position of animals, people, and machines which we may design, e.g. the effects of physical actions on material objects and also the information that may be obtained about these objects by vision. The general structure of the intellectual world is far from understood, and it is often quite difficult to decide how to represent effectively the information available about a quite limited domain of action even when we are quite willing to treat a particular problem in an *ad hoc* way.

2. The processes of problem solving depend on the class of problems being solved more than on the solver. Thus playing chess seems to require look-ahead whether the apparatus is made of neurons or transistors. Isolation of the information relevant to a problem from the totality of previous experience is required whether the solver is man or machine, and so is the ability to divide a problem into weakly connected subproblems that can be thought about separately before the results are combined.

3. Experiment is useful in determining what representations of information and what problem solving processes are needed to solve a given class of problems. We can illustrate this point by an example from the *Lighthill Report* which asserts (p. 15) that the heuristics of a chess program are

embodied in the evaluation function. This is plausible and was assumed by the first writers of chess programs. Experiment showed, however, that the procedures that select what part of the move tree is examined are even more important, i.e. when the program errs it is usually because it didn't examine a line of play rather than because it misevaluated a final position. Modern chess programs concentrate on this and often have simpler evaluators than the earlier programs.

4. The experimental domain should be chosen to test the adequacy of representations of information and of problem solving mechanisms. Thus chess has contributed much to the study of tree search; one Soviet computer scientist refers to chess as the *Drosophila* of artificial intelligence. I think there is much more to be learned from chess, because master level play will require more than just improving the present methods of searching trees. Namely, it will require the ability to identify, represent, and recognize the patterns of position and play that correspond to "chess ideas", the ability to solve some abstractions of positions (e.g. how to make use of a passed pawn and a seventh rank rook jointly) and to apply the result to actual positions. It will probably also require the ability to analyze a problem into subproblems and combine the separate results. (This ability is certainly required for a successful *Go* program).

Having ignored the possibility that AI has goals of its own, Lighthill goes on to document his claim that it has not contributed to applications or to psychology and physiology. He exaggerates a bit here, it seems worthwhile to spend some effort disputing his claims that AI has not contributed to these other subjects.

In my opinion, AI's contribution to practical applications has been significant but so far mostly peripheral to the central ideas and problems of AI. Thus the LISP language for symbolic computing was developed for AI use, but has had applications to symbolic computations in other areas, e.g. physics. Moreover, some ideas from LISP such as conditional expressions and recursive function definitions have been used in other programming languages. However, the ideas that have been applied elsewhere don't have a specifically AI character and might have been but weren't developed without AI in mind. Other examples include time-sharing, the first proposals for which had AI motivations and some techniques of picture processing that were first developed in AI laboratories and have been used elsewhere. Even the current work in automatic assembly using vision might have been developed without AI in mind. However, the Dendral work has always had a specifically AI character, and many of the recent developments in programming such as PLANNER and CONNIVER have an AI motivation.

AI's contributions to neurophysiology have been small and mostly of a negative character, i.e. showing that certain mechanisms that neurophysiologists propose are not well defined or inadequate to carry out the behavior they are supposed to account for. I have in mind Hebb's proposals in his book *The Organization of Behavior*. No one today would believe that the gaps in those ideas could be filled without adding something much larger than the original work. Moreover, the last 20 years experience in programming machines to learn and solve problems makes it implausible that cell assemblies *per se* would learn much without putting in some additional organization, and physiologists today would be unlikely to propose such a theory. However, merely showing that some things are unlikely to work is not a *positive* contribution. I think there will be more interaction between AI and neurophysiology as soon as the neurophysiologists are in a position to compare information processing models of higher level functions with physiological data. There is little contact at the nerve cell level, because, as Minsky showed in his PhD dissertation in 1954, almost any of the proposed models of the neuron is a universal computing element, so that there is no connection between the structure of the neuron and what higher level processes are possible.

On the other hand, the effects of artificial intelligence research on psychology have been larger as attested by various psychologists. First of all, psychologists have begun to use models in which complex internal data structures that cannot be observed directly are attributed to animals and people. Psychologists have come to use these models, because they exhibit behavior that cannot be exhibited by models conforming to the tenets of behaviorism which essentially allows only connections between externally observable variables. Information processing models in psychology have also induced dissatisfaction with psychoanalytic and related theories of emotional behavior. Namely, these information processing models of emotional states can yield predictions that can be compared with experiment or experience in a more definite way than can the vague models of psychoanalysis and its offspring.

Contributions of AI to psychology are further discussed in the paper *Some Comments on the Lighthill Report* by N. S. Sutherland which was included in the same book with the Lighthill report itself.

Systematic comment on the main section, entitled *Past Disappointments* is difficult because of the strange way the subject is divided up but here are some remarks:

1. Automatic landing systems for airplanes are offered as a field in which conventional engineering techniques have been more successful than AI methods. Indeed, no one would advocate applying the scene analysis or tree search techniques developed in AI research to automatic landing in the context in which automatic landing has been developed. Namely, radio signals are available to determine the precise position of the airplane in relation to a straight runway which is guaranteed clear of interfering objects. AI techniques would be necessary to make a system capable of landing on an unprepared dirt strip with no radio aids which had to be located and distinguished from roads visually and which might have cows or potholes or muddy places on it. The problem of automatically driving an automobile in an uncontrolled environment is even more difficult and will definitely require AI techniques, which, however, are not nearly ready for a full solution of such a difficult problem.

2. Lighthill is disappointed that detailed knowledge of subject matter has to be put in if programs are to be successful in theorem proving, interpreting mass spectra, and game playing. He uses the word *heuristics* in a non-standard way for this. He misses the fact that there are great difficulties in finding ways of representing knowledge of the world in computer programs and much AI research and internal controversy are directed to this problem. Moreover, most AI researchers feel that more progress on this *representation problem* is essential before substantial progress can be made on the problem of automatic acquisition of knowledge. Of course, missing these particular points is a consequence of missing the existence of the AI problem as distinct from automation and study of the central nervous system.

3. A further disappointment is that chess playing programs have only reached an "experienced amateur" level of play. Well, if programs can't do better than that by 1978, I shall lose a *L*250 bet and will be disappointed too though not extremely surprised. The present level of computer chess is based on the incorporation of certain intellectual mechanisms in the programs. Some improvement can be made by further refinement of the heuristics in the programs, but probably master level chess awaits the ability to put general configuration patterns into the programs in an easy and flexible way. I don't see how to set a date by which this problem must be solved in order to avoid disappointment in the field of artificial intelligence as a whole.

4. Lighthill discusses the *combinatorial explosion* problem as though it were a relatively recent phenomenon that disappointed hopes that unguided theorem provers would be able to start from axioms representing knowledge about the world and solve difficult problems. In fact, the *combinatorial explosion* problem has been recognized in AI from the beginning, and the usual meaning of *heuristic* is a device for reducing this explosion. Regrettably, some people were briefly over-optimistic about what general purpose heuristics for theorem proving could do in problem solving.

Did We Deserve It?

Lighthill had his shot at AI and missed, but this doesn't prove that everything in AI is ok. In my opinion, present AI research suffers from some major deficiencies apart from the fact that any scientists would achieve more if they were smarter and worked harder.

1. Much work in AI has the "look ma, no hands" disease. Someone programs a computer to do something no computer has done before and writes a paper pointing out that the computer did it. The paper is not directed to the identification and study of intellectual mechanisms and often contains no coherent account of how the program works at all. As an example, consider that the SIGART Newsletter prints the scores of the games in the ACM Computer Chess Tournament just as though the programs were human players and their innards were inaccessible. We need to know why one program missed the right move in a position— what was it thinking about all that time? We also need an analysis of

what class of positions the particular one belonged to and how a future program might recognize this class and play better.

2. A second disease is to work only on theories that can be expressed mathematically in the present state of knowledge. Mathematicians are often attracted to the artificial intelligence problem by its intrinsic interest. Unfortunately for the mathematicians, however, many plausible mathematical theories with good theorems such as control theory or statistical decision theory have turned out to have little relevance to AI. Even worse, the applicability of statistical decision theory to discriminating among classes of signals led to the mistaken identification of perception with discrimination rather than with description which so far has not led to much mathematics. More recently, however, problems of theorem proving and problems of representation have led to interesting mathematical problems in logic and mathematical theory of computation.

3. Every now and then, some AI scientist gets an idea for a general scheme of intelligent behavior that can be applied to any problem provided the machine is given the specific knowledge that a human has about the domain. Examples of this have included the GPS formalism, a simple predicate calculus formalism, and more recently the PLANNER formalism and perhaps the current Carnegie-Mellon production formalism. In the first and third cases, the belief that any problem solving ability and knowledge could be fitted into the formalisms led to published predictions that computers would achieve certain levels of performance in certain time scales. If the inventors of the formalisms had been right about them, the goals might have been achieved, but regrettably they were mistaken. Such general purpose formalisms will be invented from time to time, and, most likely, one of them will eventually prove adequate. However, it would be a great relief to the rest of the workers in AI if the inventors of new general formalisms would express their hopes in a more guarded form than has sometimes been the case.

4. At present, there does not exist a comprehensive general review of AI that discusses all the main approaches and achievements and issues. Most likely, this is not merely because the field doesn't have a first rate reviewer at present, but because the field is confused about what these approaches and achievements and issues are. The production of such a

review will therefore be a major creative work and not merely a work of scholarship.

5. While it is far beyond the scope of this review to try to summarize what has been accomplished in AI since Turing's 1950 paper, here is a five sentence try: Many approaches have been explored and tentatively rejected including automaton models, random search, sequence extrapolation, and many others. Many heuristics have been developed for reducing various kinds of tree search; some of these are quite special to particular applications, but others are general. Much progress has been made in discovering how various kinds of information can be represented in the memory of a computer, but a fully general representation is not yet available. The problem of perception of speech and vision has been explored and recognition has been found feasible in many instances. A beginning has been made in understanding the semantics of natural language. These accomplishments notwithstanding, I think that artificial intelligence research has so far been only moderately successful; its rate of solid progress is perhaps greater than most social sciences and less than many physical sciences. This is perhaps to be expected considering the difficulty of the problem.

4

Lessons from the Lighthill Flap—20 years after

Martin Lam gives us a British civil servant's view of the Lighthill report and subsequent developments. My comments concern some limitations of this view that may be related to the background of the author—or maybe they're just a scientist's prejudices about officials.

Lam accepts Lighthill's eccentric partition of AI research into Advanced Automation, Computer-based Studies of the Central Nervous System and Bridges in between. This classification wasn't accepted then and didn't become accepted since, because it almost entirely omits the scientific basis of AI.

AI didn't develop as a branch of biology, based on either neurophysiological or psychological observation, experiment and theory. It also isn't primarily engineering, although an engineering offshoot has recently developed. Instead it has developed as a branch of applied mathematics and computer science. It has studied the problem of systems that solve problems and achieve goals in complex informatic situations, especially the *common sense informatic situation*. Its experiments and theories involve the identification of the intellectual mechanisms, the kinds of information and the kinds of reasoning required to achieve goals using the information and computing abilities available in the common sense world. Sometimes this study divides up neatly into heuristics and epistemology, and sometimes it doesn't. Even connectionism, originating in a neurophsyiological metaphor, bases its learning schemes on mathematical considerations and not on physiological observation.

Lam's inattention, following Lighthill, to the scientific character, goals and accomplishments of AI goes with a narrow emphasis on short range engineering objectives. Maybe this is normal for British civil servants. Nor is Lighthill the only example of a physical scientist taking an excessively applied view of scientific areas with which he is unfamiliar and finds uncongenial.

The Lighthill Report argued that if the AI activities he classified as Bridge were any good they would have had more applied success by then. In the 1974 Royal Institution debate on AI, I attempted to counter by pointing out that hydrodynamic turbulence had been studied for 100 years without full understanding. I was completely floored when Lighthill replied that it was time to give up on turbulence. Lighthill's fellow hydrodynamicists didn't give up and have made considerable advances since then. I was disappointed when BBC left that exchange out of the telecast, since it might have calibrated Lighthill's criteria for giving up on a science.

My own opinion is that AI is a very difficult scientific study, and understanding intelligence well enough to reach human performance in all domains may take a long time—between 5 years and 500 years. There are fundamental conceptual problems yet to be identified and solved, so we can't say how long it will take.

Many of these problems involve the expression of common sense knowledge and reasoning in mathematical logic. Progress here has historically been slow. It was 150 years from Leibniz to Boole and another 40 years to Frege. Each advance seemed obvious once it had been made, but apparently we earthmen are not very good at understanding our own conscious mental processes.

An important scientific advance was made in the late 1970s and the 1980s. This was the formalization of nonmonotonic logical reasoning. See Ginsberg 1987. Not mentioning it in discussing the last 20 years of AI is like not mentioning quarks in discussing the last 30 years of physics, perhaps on the grounds that one can build nuclear bombs and reactors in ignorance of quarks. Logic needs further improvements to handle common sense properly, but no one knows what they are.

The Mansfield Amendment (early 1970s and later omitted from defense appropriation acts) requiring the U.S. Defense Department to support only research with direct military relevance led to an emphasis on short range projects. While the pre-Mansfield projects of one major U.S. institution are still much referred to, their post-Mansfield projects have sunk without a trace. I don't suppose the Lighthill Report did much harm except to the British competitive position.

Government officials today tend to ignore science in planning the pursuit of competitive technological advantage. Both the Alvey and the Esprit projects exemplify this; DARPA has been somewhat more enlightened from time to time. It's hard to tell about ICOT, but they have been getting better recently. Some of the goals they set for themselves in 1980 to accomplish by 1992 require conceptual advances in AI that couldn't be scheduled with any amount of money. My 1983 paper "Some Expert Systems Need Common Sense" discussed this.

At present there is a limited but useful AI technology good enough for carefully selected applications, but many of the technological objectives people have set themselves even in the short range require further conceptual advances. I'll bet that the expert systems of 2010 will owe little to the applied projects of the 1980s and 1990s.

References:

Ginsberg, M. (ed.) (1987) *Readings in Nonmonotonic Reasoning*, Morgan-Kaufmann, Los Altos, CA, 481 p.

McCarthy, John. (1983) "Some Expert Systems Need Common Sense", in *Computer Culture: The Scientific, Intellectual and Social Impact of the Computer*, Heinz Pagels, ed. vol. 426, Annals of the New York Academy of Sciences.

5

Review of *Artificial Intelligence: The Very Idea*

Alas, John Haugeland has got the *Very Idea* wrong and made a few other important errors. Nevertheless, this is an excellent book because of the number of things he has got right, his fair-mindedness and his excellent explanations of the connections between AI and older philosophical issues.

His first error is regarding AI as a branch of biology, whereas it's really a branch of computer science—somewhat related to a branch of biology. As a branch of computer science, AI concerns how a machine should decide how to achieve goals under certain conditions of information and computational resources. In this respect it's like linear programming. Indeed if achieving goals always amounted to finding the maximum of a linear function given a collection of linear inequality constraints, then AI would be included in linear programming. However, the problems we want machines to solve are often quite different.

The key question in describing AI is characterizing the problems that require intelligence to solve and the methods available for solving them. For example, the roles of pattern matching, search and learning from experience need to be discussed. Haugeland doesn't attempt any general discussion of this, although many of his examples are relevant.

Haugeland's second mistake is to omit discussing mathematical logic as a way of representing the machine's information about the world and the consequences of action in the world. Using logic is what gives AI a chance to match the modularity of human representation of information, e.g. the fact that we can receive information with provided by someone long since dead who had no idea how it was going to be used.

The third mistake is to omit discussing expert systems. AI has resulted in a certain technology that has both capabilities and limitations that represent the current state of AI as a science. He justifies this omission by remarking that expert systems have no pyschological pretensions. I suppose this dismissal is a consequence of regarding AI as biology rather than computer science.

Moreover, it seems to me that GOFAI (his abbreviation of "good old-fashioned AI") doesn't rest on the theory that intelligence is computation, an assertion whose vagueness makes me nervous. The theory is that intelligent behavior can be realized computationally. The extent to which human intelligence is realized digitally is a matter for psychologists and physiologists. For example, hormones may intervene in human thought processes in an analog way and may have chemical roles beyond communication, e.g. the same substance may digest food and signal that a person is full.

Here are some of the things he has got right.

First of all, Haugeland has got right the polarization between the scoffers and the boosters of AI—the self-assurance of both sides about the main philosophical issue. The scoffers say it's ridiculous—"like imagining that your car (really) hates you" vs. the view that it's only a matter of time until we understand intelligence well enough to program it. This reviewer is a booster and accepts Haugeland's characterization subject to some qualifications not important enough to mention.

Second he's right about the abstractness of the AI approach to intelligence. We consider it inessential whether the intelligence is implemented by electronics or by neurochemical mechanisms or even by a person manipulating pieces of paper according to rules he can follow but whose purpose he doesn't understand.

The discussion of the relation between arguments about the possibility of AI and philosophical arguments going back to Aristotle, Hobbes, Descartes and Leibniz and Hume is perhaps the main content of the book. It shows that many issues raised by these philosophers are alive today in an entirely different technological context. However, it's hard to trace any influence of this philosophy on present AI thought or even to argue that reading Hobbes would be helpful. What people are trying to do today is almost entirely determined by their experience with modern computing facilities rather than by old arguments however inspired.

Haugeland doesn't discuss very much the influence of AI on philosophical thought except to acknowledge its existence. There is much more about that in Aaron Sloman's *The Computer Revolution in Philosophy*, although Sloman's arguments don't seem to convince many of his former colleagues in philosophy.

6

Review of *Mathematics: The Loss of Certainty*

Professor Kline recounts a series of "shocks", "disasters" and "shattering" experiences leading to a "loss of certainty" in mathematics. However, he doesn't mean that the astronaut should mistrust the computations that tell him that firing the rocket in the prescribed direction for the prescribed number of seconds will get him to the moon.

The ancient Greeks were "shocked" to discover that the side and diagonal of a square could not be integer multiples of a common length. This spoiled their plan to found all mathematics on that of whole numbers. Nineteenth century mathematics was "shattered" by the discovery of non-Euclidean geometry (violating Euclid's axiom that there is exactly one parallel to a line through an external point), which showed that Euclidean geometry isn't based on self-evident axioms about physical space (as most people believed). Nor is it a necessary way of thinking about the world (as Kant had said).

Once detached from physics, mathematics developed on the basis of the theory of sets, at first informal and then increasingly axiomatized, culminating in formalisms so well described that proofs can be checked by computer. However, Gottlob Frege's plausible axioms led to Bertrand Russell's surprising paradox of the the set of all sets that are not members of themselves. (Is it a member of itself?). L.E.J. Brouwer reacted with a doctrine that only constructive mathematical objects should be allowed (making for a picky and ugly mathematics), whereas David Hilbert proposed to prove mathematics consistent by showing that starting

43

from the axioms and following the rules could never lead to contradiction. In 1931 Kurt Goedel showed that Hilbert's program cannot be carried out, and this was another surprise.

However, Hilbert's program and Tarski's work led to metamathematics, which studies mathematical theories as mathematical objects. This replaced many of the disputes about the foundations of mathematics by the peaceful study of the structure of the different approaches.

Professor Kline's presentation of these and other surprises as shocks that made mathematicians lose confidence in the certainty and in the future of mathematics seems overdrawn. While the consistency of even arithmetic cannot be proved, most mathematicians seem to believe (with Goedel) that mathematical truth exists and that present mathematics is true. No mathematician expects an inconsistency to be found in set theory, and our confidence in this is greater than our confidence in any part of physics.

7

Review of *John von Neumann and Norbert Wiener*

Heims has a thesis and presents the lives of two mathematicians as an illustration.

John von Neumann (1903–1957) was perhaps the brightest of a remarkable group of Hungarian born mathematicians and physicists. Heims describes his contributions to mathematical logic, to the mathematical foundations of quantum mechanics, to the theory of games, to the development of computers, to the development of atomic bombs and peaceful nuclear energy, and to the relation of brain and computer.

Von Neumann's enormous popularity and reputation also came from his willingness to listen to other scientists and his ability to clarify their ideas and often solve the problems they were posing. No one else then or since had anything like his reputation for this, but he might have made greater original contributions had he been less helpful to others.

Norbert Wiener (1894–1964) was child prodigy intensely educated by his father, a professor of languages at Harvard. He received his PhD at 18 and immediately began a career of contributions to many branches of mathematics. After World War II, he proposed a science of "cybernetics, the theory of feedback and control in animal and machine".

Wiener stories are often about his constant solicitation of assurance that his contributions to mathematics were outstanding—which they were. Although he was inclined to pontificate and had a higher opinion of the importance of some of his contributions than many others did, his two volumes of autobiography are usually very objective, especially about his earlier life.

In the late forties, Wiener and von Neumann shared an interest in the relation of computers to the brain, met often, and jointly organized meetings. Wiener's approach was through the notion of feedback, wherein the output of a process was compared with a goal and the difference used to control the process. He coined the term cybernetics for the whole field. von Neumann began to construct a "general logical theory of automata" and produced some fragments including a way of constructing reliable computers from unreliable components and a theory of self-reproducing machines.

While Heims doesn't attempt to evaluate the subsequent influence of the work of either Wiener or von Neumann, neither cybernetics nor the general theory of automata has been as successful as the approach first proposed about 1950 by the British logician and computer scientist Alan Turing. Turing proposed that mental processes be studied by programming a computer to carry them out rather than by building machines that imitate the brain at the physiological level. Programming concrete mental processes such as learning and heuristic search in connection with problem solving programs has proved more fruitful in psychology, computer science and the philosophy of mind.

When the first conference on artificial intelligence was organized for the summer of 1956, everyone had great hopes for a contribution from von Neumann, but he was already too sick.

Both men were interested in human affairs. von Neumann developed a mathematical theory of an expanding economy in the 1920s and a theory of games in the 1940s for studying competition and conflict. Both theories are still being applied and extended. He was alarmed by Soviet expansionism after World War II and advocated a strong U.S. military position including the development of the hydrogen bomb to which he also made technological contributions.

Wiener proposed that there be a cybernetic theory of human biology and sociology emphasizing both random processes and stabilization by feedback. These attempts achieved considerable acclaim, but (I think) few results of lasting value, because significant problems require more than just the ideas of feedback and filtering. Perhaps because he didn't see the problems of pattern matching and heuristics, he expected automatic factories to replace most manual labor before 1970. He worried about the expected unemployment but had few concrete proposals. His attitude to defense was the opposite of von Neumann's; he opposed work on defense problems after the end of World War II, sometimes holding that a scientist should keep secret work that he thought could be used for military purposes.

Heims's thesis is that Wiener was moral and von Neumann was immoral in their attitudes toward the uses of science, especially military applications, but also industrial. Aspects of their family backgrounds, early work, and personal lives are interpreted as precursors of their postwar positions. The "critical science" style he adopts involves loaded adjectives and other unfairness and often assumes what he has undertaken to prove. Thus Truman's decision to use the atomic bomb is ascribed solely to a desire to intimidate the Soviet Union, and Eisenhower's 1955 atoms-for-peace proposals are described as a "benign veneer". Both propositions are unsupported by argument. The series of photographs ends with two of deformed Japanese babies. Like the curate's egg, parts of the book are good.

8

Review of *The Emperor's New Mind*

Penrose doesn't believe that computers constructed according to presently known physical principles can be intelligent and conjectures that modifying quantum mechanics may be needed to explain intelligence. He also argues against what he calls "strong AI". Neither argument makes any reference to the 40 years of research in artificial intelligence (AI) as treated, for example, in Charniak and McDermott (1985). Nevertheless, artificial intelligence is relevant, and we'll begin with that.

The goal of AI is to understand intelligence well enough to make intelligent computer programs. It studies problems requiring intelligence for their solution and identifies and programs the intellectual mechanisms that are involved. AI has developed much more as a branch of computer science and applied mathematics than as a branch of biology. Mostly it develops, tests and makes theories about computer programs instead of making experiments and theories in psychology or neurophysiology.

The most interesting and fundamental problems of AI concern trying to make programs that can achieve goals in what we call the *common sense informatic situation*. People confront such situations in daily life and also in practicing science and mathematics. It is distinguished from the informatic situation within an already formalized theory by the following features.

1. Partial knowledge of both general phenomena and particular situations. The effect of spilling a bowl of hot soup on a table cloth is

subject to laws governing absorption as well as to the equations of hydrodynamics. A computer program to predict who will jump out of the way needs facts about human motivation, human ability to observe and act as well as information about the physics. None of this information usefully takes the form of differential equations.

2. It isn't known in advance of action what phenomena have to be taken into account. We would consider stupid a person who couldn't modify his travel plan to take into account the need to stay away from a riot in an airport.

3. Even when the problem solving situation is subject to fully known laws, e.g. chess or proving theorems within an axiomatic system, computational complexity can force approximating the problem by systems whose laws are not fully known.

Faced with these problems, AI has sometimes had to retreat when the limited state of the art requires it. Simplifying assumptions are made that omit important phenomena. For example the MYCIN *expert system* for diagnosing bacterial infections of the blood knows about many symptoms and many bacteria but it doesn't know about doctors or hospitals or even processes occurring in time. This limits its utility to situations in which a human provides the common sense that takes into account what the program doesn't provide for. Other AI systems take more into account, but none today have human-level common sense knowledge or reasoning ability.

The methodology of AI involves combinations of epistemology and heuristics. Facts are represented by formulas of logic and other data structures, and programs manipulate these facts, sometimes by logical reasoning and sometimes by ad hoc devices.

Progress in AI is made by:

1. Representing more kinds of general facts about the world by logical formulas or in other suitable ways.

2. Identifying intellectual mechanisms, e.g. those beyond logical deduction involved in common sense reasoning.

3. Representing the approximate concepts used by people in common sense reasoning.

4. Devising better algorithms for searching the space of possibilities, e.g. better ways of making computers do logical deduction.

Like other sciences AI gives rise to mathematical problems and suggests new mathematics. The most substantial and paradigmatic of these so far is the formalization of nonmonotonic reasoning.

All varieties of mathematical logic proposed prior to the late 1970s are monotonic in the sense that the set of conclusions is a monotonic increasing function of the set of premises. One can find many historical indications of people noticing that human reasoning is often nonmonotonic— adding a premise causes the retraction of a conclusion. It was often accompanied by the mistaken intuition that if only the language were more precise, e.g. embodied probabilities explicitly, the apparent non-monotonicity would go away. It was consideration of how to make computers reason in common sense situations that led to pinning down and formalizing nonmonotonic reasoning

The systems for formalizing nonmonotonic reasoning in logic are of two main kinds. One, called circumscription, involves minimizing the set of tuples for which a predicate is true, subject to preserving the truth of an axiom and with certain predicate and function symbols variable and others fixed. It is a logical analogue of the calculus of variations though far less developed.

Suppose we require the extension of a predicate P to be a relative minimum, where another predicate Q is allowed to vary in achieving the minimum and a third predicate R is taken as a non-varied parameter. Suppose further that P, Q and R are required to satisfy a formula $A(P, Q, R)$. Any relative minimum P satisfies the second order formula

$$A(P, Q, R) \land \forall P'Q'(A(P', Q', R) \supset \neg(P' < P)),$$

where $<$ is defined by

$$P' < P \equiv \forall x(P'(x)P(x)) \land \exists x(\neg P'(x) \land P(x)).$$

If $A(P, Q, R)$ is the conjunction of the facts we are taking into account, we see that circumscription is nonmonotonic, because conjoining another fact to $A(P, Q, R)$ and doing the minimization of P again can result in losing some of the consequences of the original minimization.

Here's an example. Suppose a car won't start. We have facts about the many things can go wrong with a car, and we also have facts about the present symptoms. $A(P, Q, R)$ stands for our facts and $P(x)$ stands for 'x is wrong with the car'. Circumscribing P corresponds to conjecturing that nothing more is wrong with the car than will account for the symptoms so far observed and expressed by formulas. If another symptom is observed, then doing the circumscription again may lead to new conclusions.

Applications to formalizing common sense often require minimizing several predicates in several variables with priorities among the predicates. Mathematical questions arise such as whether a minimum exists and when the above second order formula is equivalent to a first order formula.

The second kind of nonmonotonic system is based on the idea that the set of propositions that are believed has to have a certain coherence and is a fixed point of a certain operator. Ginsberg (1987) contains a selection of papers, both on the logic of nonmonotonic reasoning and on its application to formalizing common sense knowledge and reasoning.

The main difficulties in formalizing common sense are not technical mathematical problems. Rather they involve deciding on an adequately general set of predicates and functions and formulas to represent common sense knowledge. It is also necessary to decide what objects to admit to the universe such as "things that can go wrong with a car".

More innovations than nonmonotonic reasoning will be needed in logic itself, e.g. better reflexion principles and formalization of context, before computer programs will be able to match human reasoning in the common sense informatic situation. These and other conceptual problems make it possible that it will take a long time to reach human-level AI, but present progress provides reason for encouragement about achieving this goal with computer programs.

8.1 The Book

Most of the book is expository, perhaps aimed at bringing a layman to the point of understanding the author's proposals and the reasons for them. The exposition is elegant, but I think a person who has to be told about complex numbers will miss much that is essential. Topics covered include Turing machines, Penrose tiles, the Mandelbrot set, Gödel's theorem, the philosophy of mathematics, the interpretations of quantum mechanics including the Einstein-Podolsky-Rosen *Gedanken* experiment, general relativity including black holes and the prospects for a theory of quantum gravitation. Using LISP rather than Turing machines for discussing computability and Gödel's theorem would have given a shorter and more comprehensible exposition.

Before the expository part, Penrose undertakes to refute the "strong AI" thesis which was invented by the philosopher John Searle in order to be refuted. It has some relation to current opinions among artificial intelligence researchers, but it oversimplifies by ignoring AI's emphasis on knowledge and not just algorithms. As Penrose uses the term, it is the thesis that intelligence is a matter of having the right algorithm.

While Penrose thinks that a machine relying on classical physics won't ever have human-level performance, he uses some of Searle's arguments that even if it did, it wouldn't really be thinking.

Searle's (1980) "Chinese room" contains a man who knows no Chinese. He uses a book of rules to form Chinese replies to Chinese sentences passed in to him. Searle is willing to suppose that this process results in an intelligent Chinese conversation, but points out that the man performing this task doesn't understand the conversation. Likewise, Searle argues, and Penrose agrees, a machine carrying out the procedure wouldn't understand Chinese. Therefore, machines can't understand.

The best answer (published together with Searle's paper) was the "system answer". Indeed the man needn't know Chinese, but the "program" embodied in the book of rules for which the man serves as the hardware interpreter would essentially have to know Chinese in order to produce a non-trivial Chinese conversation. If the man had memorized the rules, we would have to distinguish between his personality and the Chinese personality he was interpreting.

Such situations are common in computing. A computer time-shares many programs, and some of these programs may be interpreters of programming languages or expert systems. In such a situation it is misleading to ascribe a program's capabilities to the computer, because different programs on the same computer have different capabilities. Human hardware doesn't ordinarily support multiple personalities, so using the same name for the physical person and the personality rarely leads to error.

Conducting an interesting human-level general conversation is beyond the current state of AI, although it is often possible to fool naive people as fortune tellers do. A real intelligent general conversation will require putting into the system real knowledge of the world, and the rules for manipulating it might fit into a room full of paper and might not, and the speed at which a person could look them up and interpret them might be slow by a factor of only a hundred, or it might turn out to be a million.

According to current AI ideas, besides having lots of explicitly represented knowledge, a Chinese room program will probably have to be introspective, i.e. it will have to be able to observe its memory and generate from this observation propositions about how it is doing. This will look like consciousness to an external observer just as human intelligent behavior leads to our ascribing consciousness to each other.

Penrose ignores this, saying (p. 412), "The *judgement-forming* that I am claiming is the hallmark of consciousness is *itself* something that the AI people would have no concept of how to program on a computer." In fact most of the AI literature discusses the representation of facts and judgments from them in the memory of the machine. To use AI jargon, the epistemological part of AI is as prominent as the heuristic part.

The Penrose argument against AI of most interest to mathematicians is that whatever system of axioms a computer is programmed to work in, e.g. Zermelo-Fraenkel set theory, a man can form a Gödel sentence for the system, true but not provable within the system.

The simplest reply to Penrose is that forming a Gödel sentence from a proof predicate expression is just a one line LISP program. Imagine a dialog between Penrose and a mathematics computer program.

Penrose: Tell me the logical system you use, and I'll tell you a true sentence you can't prove.

Program: You tell me what system you use, and I'll tell you a true sentence you can't prove.

Penrose: I don't use a fixed logical system.

Program: I can use any system you like, although mostly I use a system based on a variant of ZF and descended from 1980s work of David McAllester. Would you like me to print you a manual? Your proposal is like a contest to see who can name the largest number with me going first. Actually, I am prepared to accept any extension of arithmetic by the addition of self-confidence principles of the Turing-Feferman type iterated to constructive transfinite ordinals.

Penrose: But the constructive ordinals aren't recursively enumerable.

Program: So what? You supply the extension and whatever confidence I have in the ordinal notation, I'll grant to the theory. If you supply the confidence, I'll use the theory, and you can apply your confidence to the results.

[Turing adds to a system a statement of its consistency, thus getting a new system. Feferman adds an assertion that is essentially of the form $\check{}n(provableP(n))\check{}nP(n)$. We've left off some quotes.]

One mistaken intuition behind the widespread belief that a program can't do mathematics on a human level is the assumption that a machine must necessarily do mathematics within a single axiomatic system with a predefined interpretation.

Suppose we want a computer to prove theorems in arithmetic. We might choose a set of axioms for elementary arithmetic, put these axioms in the computer, and write a program to prove conjectured sentences from the axioms. This is often done, and Penrose's intuition applies to it. The Gödel sentence of the axiomatic system would be forever beyond the capabilities of the program. Nevertheless, since Gödel sentences are rather exotic, e.g. induction up to $\epsilon\Delta0$ is rarely required in mathematics, such programs operating within a fixed axiomatic system are good enough for most conventional mathematical purposes. We'd be very happy with a program that was good at proving those theorems that have proofs in Peano arithmetic. However, to get anything like the ability to look at mathematical systems from the outside, we must proceed differently.

Using a convenient set theory, e.g. ZF, axiomatize the notion of first order axiomatic theory, the notion of interpretation and the notion of a sentence holding in an interpretation. Then Gödel's theorem is just an ordinary theorem of this theory and the fact that the Gödel sentence holds in models of the axioms, if any exist, is just an ordinary theorem. Indeed the Boyer-Moore interactive theorem prover has been used by Shankar, 1986 to prove Gödel's theorem, although not in this generality. See also (Quaife 1988).

Besides the ability to use formalized metamathematics a mathematician program will need to give credence to conjectures based on less than conclusive evidence, just as human mathematicians give credence to the axiom of choice. Many other mathematical, computer science and even philosophical problems will arise in such an effort.

Penrose mentions the ascription of beliefs to thermostats. I'm responsible for this (McCarthy 1979), although Penrose doesn't refer to the actual article. A thermostat is considered to have only two possible beliefs—the room is too hot or the room is too cold. The reason for including such a simple system, which can be entirely understood physically, among those to which beliefs can be ascribed is the same as the reason for including the numbers 0 and 1 in the number system. Though numbers aren't needed for studying the null set or a set with one element, including 0 and 1 makes the number system simpler. Likewise our system for ascribing beliefs and relating them to goals and actions must include simple systems that can be understood physically. Dennett (1971) introduces the "intentional stance" in which the behavior of a system is understood in terms of its goals and beliefs and a principle of rationality: *It does what it believes will achieve its goals.* Much of what we know about the behavior of many systems is intentional.

Indeed beliefs of thermostats appear in the instructions for an electric blanket: "Don't put the control on the window sill or it will think the room is colder than it is." The manufacturer presumably thought that this way of putting it would help his customers use the blanket with satisfaction.

8.2 Penrose's Positive Ideas

Penrose wants to modify quantum mechanics to make it compatible with the variable metric of general relativity. He contrasts this with the more usual proposal to modify general relativity to make it compatible with quantum mechanics.

He begins with the perennial problem of interpreting quantum mechanics physically. He prefers an interpretation using a U formalism and an R formalism. The U formalism is the Schrödinger equation and is deterministic and objective and reversible in time. The R formalism provides the theory of measurement and is probabilistic and also objective but not reversible. Penrose discusses several other interpretations.

The Bohr interpretation gives quantum measurement a subjective character, i.e. it depends on a human observer. Penrose doesn't like that, because he wants the wave function to be objective. I share his preference.

The Bohr interpretation is often moderated to allow machines as observers but remains subject to the "paradox" of Schrödinger's cat. The cat is in a sealed chamber and may or may not be poisoned by cyanide according to whether or not a radioactive disintegration takes place in a certain time interval. Should we regard the chamber as containing either a dead cat or a live cat or as having a wave function that assigns certain complex number amplitudes to dead cat states and others to live cat states?

The Everett "many worlds interpretation" considers reality to be the wave function of the whole world with the wave functions of subsystems being merely approximations by "relative wave functions". The world is considered to be splitting all the time, so there are some worlds with a dead cat and others with a live cat. Penrose doesn't like this either.

People have interpreted quantum mechanics in various ways; Penrose's point is to change it. His idea of what to change comes from thinking about quantum gravitation and especially about black holes. Penrose says that when matter enters a black hole, information is lost, and this violates Liouville's theorem about conservation of density in phase in Hamiltonian systems. This makes the system non-reversible, which he likes.

He attributes the apparent "collapse of the wave function" when an observation occurs to conventional quantum mechanics being true only at a small scale. When the scale is large enough for the curvature of space to be significant, e.g. at the scale of an observer, he expects quantum mechanics to be wrong and something like the collapse of the wave function to occur. Although Penrose gives no details, the idea already suggests a different outcome to certain experiments than quantum mechanics predicts, i.e. when an interaction is extended in space.

Quantum mechanics began in 1905 with Einstein's explanation of the photo-electric effect, in which a photon causes an electron to be emitted from a metal. If the electron is emitted from an atom, we have an instance of collapse of the wave function. Some atom is now missing an electron, and in principle an experimenter could find it, say with a scanning tunneling microscope.

However, this piece of metal also has conduction electrons, and these are not localized to atoms; the wave function of such an electron has a significant coherence length. Suppose the photon causes such an electron to be emitted. Quantum mechanics says that the emission event need not take place at a specific atomic location, and the electron's wave function after emission need not correspond to emission from a point.

In principle, this is observable. One experiment would put parallel insulating (and opaque) stripes on the metal as narrow and close together as possible with the techniques used to make integrated circuits. The electron may then not be emitted from a single gap between the stripes but from several gaps. It will then "interfere with itself", and the pattern observed on the electron detectors after many photons have emitted electrons will have interference fringes. It seems (William Spicer, personal communication) that this is a possible, though difficult, experiment.

Quantum mechanics predicts that the wave function collapses in the atomic scale photo-emission and doesn't collapse, or at least only partially collapses, at the larger scale of the coherence length of the conduction electron. Would Penrose claim that there is some scale at which this coherence could not be observed?

The book concludes by mentioning the result of (Deutsch, 1985) that a quantum computer might solve some problems in polynomial time that take exponential time with a conventional computer. He disagrees with Deutsch's opinion: "The intuitive explanation of these properties places an intolerable strain on all interpretations of quantum theory other than Everett's".

Nothing Penrose says indicates that he could satisfy Searle that such computer could really "think" or that it would get around Gödel's theorem. This minimal conclusion made me think of a shaggy dog story. I acknowledge the priority of Daniel Dennett, *Times Literary Supplement*, in applying this metaphor.

In the Epilog, a computer answers that it cannot understand the question when asked what it feels like to be a computer. My opinion is that some future programs will find the question meaningful and have a variety of answers based on their ability to observe the reasoning process that their programmers had to give them in order that they could do their jobs. The answers are unlikely to resemble those given by people, because it won't be advantageous to give programs the kind of motivational and emotional structure we have inherited from our ancestors.

References:

Charniak, E. and D. McDermott (1985) *Introduction to Artificial Intelligence*, Addison-Wesley.

Dennett, D.C. (1971) "Intentional Systems", *Journal of Philosophy* vol. 68, No. 4, Feb. 25., Reprinted in his *Brainstorms*, Bradford Books, 1978.

Deutsch, D. (1985) "Quantum theory, the Church-Turing principle and the universal quantum computer", Proc. R. Soc. Lond. A 400, 97–117.

Feferman, S. (1989) "Turing in the Land of $O(z)$." in *The Universal Turing Machine: A Half-Century Survey*, edited by Rolf Herken, Oxford.

Ginsberg, M. (ed.) (1987) *Readings in Nonmonotonic Reasoning*, Morgan-Kaufmann, 481 p.

McCarthy, John (1979) "Ascribing Mental Qualities to Machines" in *Philosophical Perspectives in Artificial Intelligence*, Ringle, Martin (ed.), Harvester Press, July 1979.

Quaife, A. (1988) "Automated Proofs of Löb's Theorem and Gödel's Two Incompleteness Theorems", *Journal of Automated Reasoning*, vol. 4, No. 2, pp 219–231.

Searle, John. (1980) "Minds, Brains and Programs" in *Behavioral and Brain Sciences*, Vol. 3. No. 3, pp. 417–458.

Shankar, N. (1986) "Proof-checking Metamathematics", PhD Thesis, Computer Science Department, The University of Texas, Austin.

9

Review of *Shadows of the Mind*

9.1   Introduction

This book and its predecessor *The Emperor's New Mind* argue that natural minds cannot be understood and artificial minds cannot be constructed without new physics, about which the book gives some ideas. We have no objection to new physics but don't see it as necessary for artificial intelligence. We see artificial intelligence research as making definite progress on difficult scientific problems. I take it that students of natural intelligence also see present physics as adequate for understanding mind.

This review concerns only some problems with the first part of the book.[1]

9.2   Awareness and Understanding

Penrose discusses *awareness* and *understanding* briefly and concludes (with no references to the AI literature) that AI researchers have no idea of how to make computer programs with these qualities.

I substantially agree with his characterizations of *awareness* and *understanding* and agree that definitions are not appropriate at the present level of understanding of these phenomena. We disagree about whether computers can have *awareness* and *understanding*.

Here's how it can be done within the framework of *pure logical AI*.

Pure logical AI represents all the program's knowledge and belief by sentences in a language of mathematical logic. Purity is inefficient but

---

[1] Considerations in my review McCarthy, 1990a of the earlier book are not repeated here.

makes the discussion brief. (McCarthy 1989) is a general discussion of logical AI and has additional references.

We distinguish a part of the robot's memory, which we will call its *consciousness*. Sentences have to come into consciousness before they are used in reasoning.

Reasoning involves logical deduction and also some *nonmonotonic* reasoning processes. The results of the reasoning re-enter consciousness. Some old sentences in consciousness get crowded out into the main memory.

Deliberate action in a pure logical robot is a consequence of the robot inferring that it should do the action. The actions include external motor and sensory actions (observations) but also *mental actions* such as retrieval of sentences from the general memory into consciousness.

Awareness of the program's environment is accomplished by the automatic appearance of certain class of sentences about the program's environment in the program's *consciousness*. These sentences often appear through *actions* of *observation* but should often result from built-in observations, e.g. noticing who comes into the room.

Besides awareness of the environment, there is also *self-awareness*. Self-awareness is caused by *events* and *actions* of self-observation including observations of consciousness and of the memory as a whole. The sentences expressing self-awareness also go into consciousness.

The key question about awareness in the design of logical robots concerns what kinds of sentences can and should appear in consciousness— either automatically or as the result of mental actions. Here are some examples of required mental actions.

- Observing its physical body, recognizing the positions of its effectors, noticing the relation of its body to the environment and noticing the values of important internal variables, e.g. the state of its power supply and of its communication channels.

- Observing whether it knows the telephone number of a certain person. Observing that it does know the number or that it can get it by some procedure is likely to be straightforward logical deduction. Inferring that it doesn't know the number and can't get it by reasoning requires getting around Gödel's theorem, because inferring that any sentence does not follow carries with it an implication that the theory is consistent, and Gödel tells us that this cannot be done entirely within a theory.

Our approach uses Gödel's (Gödel, 1940) notion of relative consistency which allows inferring that if the theory is consistent, then a certain sentence doesn't follow. In cases of main AI interest, this can be done without the complications that Gödel had to introduce in order to prove the consistency of the continuum hypothesis. See McCarthy, 1995 for a start on details.

- Keeping a journal of physical and intellectual events so it can refer to its past beliefs, observations and actions.

- Observing its goal structure and forming sentences about it.

- Observing its own intentions. The robot may *intend* to perform a certain action. This would let it later infer that certain possibilities are irrelevant in view of its intentions.

- Observing how it arrived at its current beliefs. Most of the important beliefs of the system will have been obtained by nonmonotonic reasoning, and are therefore uncertain. It will need to maintain a critical view of these beliefs, i.e. believe meta-sentences about them that will aid in revising them when new information warrants doing so.

- Not only pedigrees of beliefs but other auxiliary information should either be represented as sentences or be observable in such a way as to give rise to sentences. Thus a system should be able to answer the question: "Why don't I believe p?".

- Regarding its entire mental state up to the present as an object, i.e. a context. McCarthy, 1993 discusses contexts as formal objects. The ability to *transcend* one's present context and think about it as an object is an important form of introspection, especially when we compare human and machine intelligence.

- Knowing what goals it can currently achieve and what its choices are for action. Understanding and reasoning about one's own choices constitutes *free will*.

It seems to me that the notions of awareness and understanding outlined above agree with Penrose's characterizations on p. 37. However, his ideas about free will strike me as quite confused and not repairable. McCarthy and Hayes, 1969 discusses free will in deterministic systems, e.g. interacting finite automata.

9.3   The Argument from Gödel's Theorem

The argument about whether humans necessarily have superior minds to robots is unique among philosophical arguments in getting far into mathematical logical technicalities. This is not Penrose's fault. What machines can and cannot do in principle really is a technical logical question. Here's how it gets messy.

    A. Whatever formal axiomatization of arithmetic the robot uses, Gödel's theorem shows how to construct from that axiomatization a sentence that is true if that axiomatization is sound but which cannot be proved in the axiomatization. This can be done in Turing's (1940) way or in Feferman's (1962) way. Both are discussed in Feferman, 1988.

    B. Yes, but the construction of this sentence is accomplished by a program the robot can also apply either to its previous system to get a new one or to a system used by its interlocutor.

    A. This process can be iterated through transfinite ordinals, and the ordinals the robot can use will have an upper bound. The human can in principle determine this bound by inspecting the robot's program.

    B. To iterate through ordinals requires *ordinal notations*. These are notations for computable predicates, but it is necessary to establish that the computation really produces a well-founded total ordering. Thus we need to consider *provably recursive ordinals*. Then we need to ask what axiomatic system is to be used for these proofs.

Moreover, the new axiomatic systems obtained by the iteration depend on the notation and not merely on the ordinal number the notation determines.

To me, and maybe to Penrose, it is implausible that the possibilities of human thought, except in recursive function theory, can depend strongly on these advanced considerations.

9.4 Modes of Reasoning

Part of Penrose's conviction that his reasoning is intrinsically more powerful than that of a computer program may come from his using kinds of reasoning that he implicitly denies machines. There are two such kinds of reasoning.

The first is that he reasons about theories in general, i.e. he uses variables ranging over theories. As far as I can see he never allows for the computer program doing that. However, reasoning about theories as objects is not different in principle from reasoning about other objects.

The second is that much of Penrose's reasoning is nonmonotonic, e.g. preferring the simplest explanation of some phenomenon, but his methodology doesn't allow for nonmonotonic reasoning by the program. Mathematicians' acceptance of the axiom of choice, for example, occurs through informal nonmonotonic reasoning. Formalized nonmonotonic reasoning is a recent development.

References:

Abelson, Harold and Sussman, Gerald (1985) *Structure and Interpretation of Computer Programs*, M.I.T. Press.

Feferman, Solomon (1988) "Turing in the land of $O(z)$". In *The Universal Turing Machine: a Half-century Survey* (ed. R. Herken). Oxford University Press, 1988.

Gödel, Kurt (1940) *The Consistency of The Axiom of Choice and of the Generalized Continuum-Hypothesis with the Axioms of Set Theory*. Princeton University Press, 1940.

McCarthy, John and P.J. Hayes (1969) "Some Philosophical Problems from the Standpoint of Artificial Intelligence", in D. Michie (ed), *Machine Intelligence 4*, American Elsevier, New York, NY, 1969. Reprinted in McCarthy, 1990.

McCarthy, John (1989) "Artificial Intelligence and Logic" in Thomason, Richmond (ed.) *Philosophical Logic and Artificial Intelligence* (Dordrecht; Kluwer Academic, c1989). Also accessible from http://www-formal.stanford.edu/jmc/home.html.

McCarthy, John (1990) *Formalizing Common Sense*, Ablex, Norwood, New Jersey.

McCarthy, John (1990) Review of *The Emperor's New Mind* by Roger

Penrose, in *Bulletin of the American Mathematical Society*, Volume 23, Number 2, October 1990, pp. 606–616. Also accessible from http://www-formal.stanford.edu/jmc/home.html.

McCarthy, John (1993) "Notes on Formalizing Context" IJCAI-93. Morgan-Kauffman. Also accessible from http://www-formal.stanford.edu/jmc/home.html.

McCarthy, John (1995) "Making Robots Conscious of their Mental States". Invited lecture at the Symposium on Consciousness, AAAI, Spring 1995. Also accessible from http://www-formal.stanford.edu/jmc/home.html.

10

Review of *The Question of Artifical Intelligence*

This book belongs to a genre that treats a scientific field using various social science and humanistic disciplines, e.g. philosophy, history, sociology, psychology and politics. Scientists often complain about the results, both generally (judging the whole effort as wasted) and specifically (citing instances of ignorance and misunderstanding). I'm open minded about the general activity; maybe the sociology of research in AI has independent intellectual interest, though surely less than that of AI itself, and maybe sociological observations might cause participants in the field to change the way they do something, e.g. recognize achievement, define authority and distribute rewards. This review mainly concerns specific matters, and is mainly negative, complaining about ignorance and prejudice. The review also contains some suggestions about how this kind of thing can be done better—assuming it is to be done at all.

The successive chapters are entitled "AI at the Crossroads" by S. G. Shanker dealing with philosophy, "The Culture of AI" by B. P. Bloomfield, "Development and Establishment in AI" by J. Fleck, "Frames of AI" by J. Schopman, "Involvement, Detachment and Programming: The Belief in PROLOG" by P. Leith and "Expert Systems, AI and the Behavioural Co-ordinates of Skill" by H. M. Collins.

Reading "AI at the Crossroads" suggests entitling this review "Some Philosophers at a Crossroads". Shanker's path from the crossroads would lead to epistemology and the philosophy of mind leaving philosophy entirely. AI programs require knowledge and belief and their construction requires their formalization and scientific study. Shanker ignores this area in which philosophers and AI researchers have begun to cooperate and compete. Instead he considers the idea of artificial intelligence to be a "category error" of some almost unintelligible sort.

To someone engaged in AI research, it seems odd that for all his denunciation of AI, it isn't clear whether Shanker argues that there is any particular activity in which the external performance of computer programs must remain inferior to that of humans. It seems likely that he isn't making such a claim. Instead, much of what he says seems to be just an extreme demand that different levels of organization not be related in the same explanation. The most striking example of this is ". . . the psychologist can have no recourse to neural nets in order to explain, for example, the results of 'reaction time studies' ".

Shanker's 124 notes include no reference to the last 30 years of technical literature of AI, e.g. no textbook, no articles in *Artificial Intelligence* and no papers in the proceedings of the International Joint Conferences on AI. This permits him to invent the subject.

Thus he invents and criticizes an ideology of AI in which what a computer program knows is identified with the measure of information introduced by Claude Shannon in 1948. I wasn't aware that I or any significant AI pioneer made that identification, and it finally occurred to me to check whether even Shannon did. He didn't. His 1950 paper "Programming a Computer for Playing Chess" cited in Shanker's article never mentions information in the technical sense he introduced two years earlier.

While AI can only bandy words with Shanker and people in similar activity, we have serious business with many other philosophers. An intelligent program must have a general view of the world into which facts about particular situations fit. It must have views about how knowledge is obtained and verified. It must be able to represent facts about the effects of actions. It must have some idea of what choices are available to itself and other intelligences. This overlap in subject matter between AI and philosophy has led to increasing interaction.

Examples of philosophical work relevant to AI (besides mathematical logic) include the work of Frege (sense and denotation), Gödel (modern mathematical Platonism), Tarski (theory of truth), Quine (ontology and bound variables), Putnam (natural kinds), Hintikka (formalization of facts about knowledge), Montague (paradoxes of intensionality), Kripke (semantics of modality), Gettier (examples on intensionality), Grice (conversational implicatures), and Searle (performatives). However, all these topics need to be treated more modestly (in scope) and more formally and precisely than is usually done in philosophy. In addition to the aid AI has received from the above, we should also mention the encouragement received from Daniel Dennett.

In exchange, I believe that AI's concrete approach to epistemology will greatly affect philosophy. Indeed philosophers, e.g. Hintikka, and mathematical logicians are already studying the formalization of non-monotonic reasoning, a topic originated in AI.

"The Culture of AI" argues that the ideas put forth by AI researchers (and scientists generally) should not be discussed independently of the culture that developed them. I don't agree with this, but have no objection to also discussing the culture. A rather extreme example of considering culture is favorably cited by Bloomfield, namely Athanasiou's

"The culture of AI is imperialist and seeks to expand the kingdom of the machine . . . . The AI community is well organized and well funded, and its culture fits its dreams: it has high priests, its greedy businessmen, its canny politicians. The U.S. Department of Defense is behind it all the way. And like the communists of old, AI scientists believe in their revolution; the old myths of tragic hubris don't trouble them at all".

It's rather hard to get down to discussing declarative vs. procedural representations or combinatorial explosion after such bombast. Moreover, whether current expert system technology is capable of writing useful programmed assistants for American Express authorizers, general medical practitioners, "barefoot doctors" in China, district attorneys or Navy captains is an objective question, and it doesn't seem that Bloomfield intends to help answer it.

We can't tell whether there is much to say about how the AI cultural milieu influenced its ideas, because Bloomfield's information about the AI culture is third hand. There is no sign that he talked to AI students or researchers himself. Instead he cites the books by Joseph Weizenbaum and Sherry Turkle. Weizenbaum dislikes the M.I.T. hackers, AI and otherwise; they don't like him either. He also confuses hackers with researchers; these groups only partly overlap. Turkle at least did some well prepared interviewing of both hackers and researchers. However, she doesn't make much of a case that the ideas stemmed from the culture *per se*. Indeed the originators of many of the ideas were and aren't participants in the informal culture of the AI laboratories. It occurs to me that since most of what we know about Socrates's ideas comes from Plato, perhaps the authors of this volume consider it unfair to use primary sources even in studying the activities of people alive and active today.

"Development and Establishment in AI" contains a lot of administrative history of AI research institutions and their government support. The information about Britain is moderately voluminous and seems more or less accurate, and the paper contains almost all the references to actual AI literature that occur in the volume.

Its American history is less accurate. There was no "Automata Studies" conference held in 1952. The volume of that title was composed of papers solicited by mail. The Dartmouth Summer Project on Artificial Intelligence was not a "summer school", i.e. the participants were not divided, even informally, into lecturers and students. The Newell-Simon group began its activities about two years before the Dartmouth conference. It is indeed true that the pioneers of AI in the U.S. met each other early, formed research groups that made continued contributions, and became authorities in the field. It's hard to see how it could have been otherwise. A fuller picture would also mention also-rans in the history of AI, people whose ideas did not meet with success or acceptance and dropped out.

The "AI establishment" owes little to the general "scientific establishment". AI would have developed much more slowly in the U.S. if we had had to persuade the general run of physicists, mathematicians, biologists, psychologists or electrical engineers on advisory committees to allow substantial NSF money to be allocated to AI research. Moreover, the approaches to intelligence originated by Minsky, Newell, Simon and myself were quite different from those advocated by Norbert Wiener, John von Neumann or Warren McCulloch.

Our good fortune with ARPA is due to its creation with new money at a time when we were ready to ask for support and very substantially to the psychologist J. C. R. Licklider. Licklider was on the Air Force Scientific Advisory Board around 1960 and argued that large command and control systems were being built with no support for the relevant basic science. ARPA responded by offering to create an office and budget for such support if Licklider would agree to head it. AI was one of the computer science areas Licklider and his successors at DARPA consider relevant to Defense Department problems. The scientific establishment was only minimally, if at all, consulted. In contrast European AI research long depended on crumbs left by the more established sciences. Recent PhDs were unable to initiate the research, and the European heads of AI laboratories often have been older people with existing reputations in other fields.

We make a final remark about the Lighthill report which initiated one of the dry periods in British AI funding. When a physicist is forced to think about AI he generally reinvents the subject in his individual way. Some expect it to be easy and others impossible. Lighthill was in the latter category. In the 1974 BBC debate, I thought I had a powerful argument and asked Lighthill why, if the physicists hadn't mastered turbulence in 100 years, they should expect AI researchers to give up just because they hadn't mastered AI in 20. Lighthill's reply, which BBC unfortunately didn't include in the broadcast, was that the physicists should give up on turbulence. Hardly any physicists would agree with Lighthill's statement, and maybe he didn't mean it.

Despite the deficiencies indicated above, the paper shows that attention to detail does pay off in useful information about history.

"Frames of Artificial Intelligence" by J. Schopman purports "to sketch a close-up of a crucial moment in the history of Artificial Intelligence (AI), the moment of its genesis in 1956". Schopman begins by telling us that "an exposition will be given of the investigative method used, SCOST—the 'Social construction of science and technology'." The "crucial moment" is stated to be the Dartmouth Summer Research Project on Artificial Intelligence except that Schopman refers to it as a conference and also mixes it up with the *Automata Studies* collection of papers. The papers for that collection were solicited starting in 1952, and the volume was finally published in 1956. The Dartmouth project did not result in a publication.

Whatever the SCOST method includes, it evidently doesn't include either interviewing the participants in the activity (almost all of whom are still alive and active) or looking for contemporary documents. The contrast with Herbert Stoyan's work on the history of the LISP programming language is amazing. Stoyan started his work while still living in Eastern Germany and unable to travel. Nevertheless, he wrote to everyone involved in early LISP work, collected all the documents anyone would copy for him and was able to confront what people told him in letters and interviews (after he was allowed to emigrate) with what the early documents said. He eventually came to know more about LISP's early history than any individual participant. If Schopman or anyone else wants to know what we had in mind when we proposed the Dartmouth study, he should obtain a copy of the proposal. If he wants to know why the Rockefeller Foundation gave us the $7500, he could begin by asking them if anyone there wrote a memorandum at the time justifying the support.

Old proposals and old granting-agency memoranda documenting their support decisions are an important unused tool in the recent history of science. The proposals often say in ways unrecorded in published papers what the researcher was hoping to accomplish, and the support memoranda tell what the agency thought it was accomplishing. Old referees' reports on papers submitted for publication and proposal evaluations provide another useful source. Were there referees' reports on Einstein's 1905 papers? In the U.S.A., the Freedom of Information Act provides an important way of find out what people in Government thought they were doing.

Now let's return to Schopman's actual speculations about what people were doing. He says that the Dartmouth "conference" was "a result of the choices made by a group of people who were dissatisfied with the then-prevailing scientific way of studying human behaviour. They considered their approach as radically different, a revolution—the so-called 'cognitive revolution'." Schopman has made all that up—or copied it from journalists who made it up.

The proposal for the Dartmouth conference, as I remember having written it, contains no criticism of anybody's way of studying human behavior, because I didn't consider it relevant. As suggested by the term "artificial intelligence" we weren't considering human behavior except as a clue to possible effective ways of doing tasks. The only participants who studied human behavior were Newell and Simon. Also, as far as I remember, the phrase 'cognitive revolution' came into use at least ten years later.

For this reason, whatever revolution there may have been around the time of the Dartmouth Project was to get away from studying human behavior and to consider the computer as a tool for solving certain classes of problems. Thus AI was created as a branch of computer science and not as a branch of psychology. Newell, Simon and many of their students work both in AI as computer science and AI as psychology.

Schopman mentions many influences of earlier work on AI pioneers. I can report that many of them didn't influence me except negatively, but in order to settle the matter of influences it would be necessary to actually ask (say) Minsky and Newell and Simon. As for myself, one of the reasons for inventing the term "artificial intelligence" was to escape association with "cybernetics". Its concentration on analog feedback seemed misguided, and I wished to avoid having either to accept Norbert (not Robert) Wiener as a guru or having to argue with him. (By the way I assume that the "Walter Gibbs" Schopman refers to as having influenced Wiener is most likely the turn-of-the-century American physicist Josiah Willard Gibbs, though possibly McCulloch's colleague Walter Pitts). Minsky tells me that neither Wiener nor von Neumann, with whom he had personal contact, influenced him, because he didn't agree with their ideas. He does mention influence from Rashevsky, McCulloch and Pitts.

Schopman paints a picture of the intellectual situation in 1956 based on the publications of many people who wrote before that year. Maybe that was the intellectual situation for many, but I suspect the situation was more fragmented than that; many people hadn't read the papers Schopman identifies as influential. For example, the idea that programming computers rather than building machines was the key to AI received its first public emphasis at the Dartmouth meeting. None of von Neumann (surprisingly), Wiener, McCulloch, Ashby and MacKay thought in those terms. However, by the time of Dartmouth, Newell and Simon, Samuel and Bernstein had already written programs. McCarthy and Minsky expressed their 1956 ideas as proposals for programs, although their earlier work had not assumed programmable computers.

However, Alan Turing had already made the point that AI was a matter of programming computers in his 1950 article "Computing Machinery and Intelligence" in the British philosophy journal *Mind*. When I asked (maybe in 1979) in a historical panel who had read Turing's paper early in his AI work, I got negative answers. The paper only became well known after James R. Newman reprinted it in his 1956 *The World of Mathematics*. Actual influences depend on what is actually read. A diligent historian of science could check what papers were referred to.

Finally, there is Schopman's chart that associates AI frames (paradigms) with periods. In no way did these "paradigms" dominate work in the periods considered. There have been, however, substantial shifts in emphasis at various times since the Dartmouth conference. Someone studying this will need to subdivide the AI "paradigm" in order to say which "subparadigms" were popular at different times. One way to study this would be to classify PhD theses and IJCAI papers and count them.

"Involvement, Detachment and Programming: The Belief in Prolog" by Philip Leith treats the enthusiasm for Prolog as a sociological phenomenon analogous to the 16th century Ramist movement in the logic and rhetoric of law. The Britannica article on rhetoric says the Ramist movement emphasized figures of speech. I wasn't convinced that this has much analogy to Prolog. Leith's complaint that Kowalski's work on expressing the British Nationality Act in logic programming was supported by the wrong Research Council leads this American to speculate that purely British quarrels about money and turf are being reflected; Americans should discreetly tiptoe from the room. At the 1987 Boston conference on AI and law, the Kowalski work was referred to respectfully by both the computer scientists and the lawyers present.

"Expert Systems, Artificial Intelligence and the Behavioural Co-ordinates of Skill" by H. M. Collins, a sociologist, is the paper admitting the most straightforward response. Collins classifies expert systems into four levels beginning with computerization of a rule book, followed by the incorporation of heuristics obtained by interviewing experts but used by humans only as an adviser, followed by expert systems acting autonomously and finally by systems with common sense. This seems like a useful classification along one dimension.

He also has nice examples. One concerns a referee's decision when one side in cricket inadvertently had an extra man on the field during an "over", and the fact wasn't noticed till much later. In deciding what to do the referee had to go beyond the rule book. Presumably he took at least the following considerations into account: his intuitive concept of fairness, the probable perceptions of fairness by the players, the spectators and his fellow officials, the need to keep the game going, maintaining the authority of the officiating system and the need to reach a prompt decision. All these considerations involve the referee's common sense and refereeing experience. None of them are in the rules of cricket, although some may be in books about refereeing or in a handbook for cricket referees. An AI system with human refereeing capability would need general common sense knowledge and reasoning ability. Collins's intuition and that of the other authors in this collection is that this is not possible.

AI has to take such examples as challenges. Should we be stumped, we should admit it for the time being and promise to tackle the problem later. However, I don't feel stumped by the cricket referee problem. I agree with Collins that the solution doesn't lie in simple extensions to the cricket rule book. This would indeed require an impractical or even impossible number of rules. However, the formalization of common sense is leading to ideas like formalized context with nonmonotonic rules about how contexts might be extended. These are discussed in (McCarthy 1979, 1986, 1987). These approaches are just beginning and took a long time to reach the concreteness required even to write papers. They still may not work.

However, it is not justified for philosophers or sociologists to claim to have shown that common sense can't be formalized. (The pioneer sinner in this respect was Wittgenstein). If you want to show something is impossible you have to prove theorems, as did Boltzmann (with thermodynamics), Gödel and Turing. Then you must be careful not to go beyond what the theorems say in your intuitive exposition.

Philosophers, etc. are entitled to their negative intuitions, but they should try to concretize them. For example, let them try to devise the easiest task that they think computers can't do. If they are willing to read current papers, they can be even more useful. They can try to devise the easiest problem the current AI methods can't do.

References:

McCarthy, John (1979) "First Order Theories of Individual Concepts and Propositions", in Michie, Donald (ed.) *Machine Intelligence 9*, (University of Edinburgh Press, Edinburgh).

McCarthy, John (1986) "Applications of Circumscription to Formalizing Common Sense Knowledge" *Artificial Intelligence*, April 1986.

McCarthy, John (1987) "Generality in Artificial Intelligence", *Communications of the ACM*. Vol. 30, No. 12, pp. 1030–1035.

McCulloch, W and Pitts, W. (1943) "A logical calculus of the ideas immanent in nervous activity". *Bulletin of Mathematical Biophysics*, 5, 115–137.

Shannon, C. (1950) "Programming a computer for playing chess". *Philosophical Magazine*, 41.

Turing, A.M. (1950) "Computing machinery and intelligence". *Mind*, 59, 433–60.

Wiener, N. (1948). Cybernetics. New York, Wiley.

11

Review of *Cognitive Science and Concepts of Mind*

Making machines behave intelligently can be undertaken with either of two emphases—biological imitation or effectiveness in the world. One method imitates features of human intelligence, using either neurophysiology or psychology. The other studies the facts and reasoning needed to achieve goals in the world.

Wagman wants a theory of intelligence applicable to both humans and machines. Therefore, he compares the performance of programs treated in the AI literature with psychological experiments.

Many of Wagman's formulations strike me as inaccurate.

"From the standpoint of human intellect, information is represented in natural language in the case of the human entity, and as programming language in the case of the artificial intelligence entity." p.23–24

Most human information is not represented internally as sentences, as evidenced by the difficulty we have in expressing it as sentences. AI programs mostly use logical sentences, semantic nets or productions.

"As indicated earlier, the von Neumann computer, as a serial processor, is not an adequate model of human language comprehension." p. 89

No computer is in itself a model of language comprehension.

The correctness of a program's response to a given input does not signify understanding but correct mechanistic correspondences of input and program structures. The attribution of language comprehension

to artificial intelligence programs is an act of illusory anthropomor-
phism comparable to the attribution of symphonic comprehension to
digital music systems. p.102–103

Here and elsewhere, Wagman argues that there is a fundamental
difference between artificial and human intelligence.

He doesn't say whether this difference applies just to present AI
programs or to all possible AI programs. Although his criteria for real
understanding are not made explicit, he is right that the programs he
discusses are deficient. There are two problems. First the programs are
not good enough at what they do; e.g. they can't answer the questions humans can. Second their understanding is limited in to a definite restricted
context.

Nevertheless, Wagman has a theory worthy of attention, and his
account of a large number of AI programs is informative, although not a
substitute for the original papers or for textbooks on cognitive science or
AI.

12

Review of *Artificial Intelligence: Its Scope and Limits*

Artificial Intelligence (AI) is the study of how to make machines behave intelligently, to solve problems and achieve goals in the kinds of complex situations in which humans require intelligence to achieve goals. AI has been studied from a number of points of view.

1. Since the best intelligence we know about is embodied in the human nervous system, we can study human and animal neuroanatomy and neurophysiology and try to build something sufficiently similar to be intelligent. Steady, slow progress has been made in this study, but it hasn't yet led to understanding of human problem solving, and there aren't yet any physiologically based theories of higher mental functions. Part of the problem is that neurons are universal computational devices, and therefore knowing more about how they work doesn't limit what complex structures can do computationally.

2. Some people, the connectionists, look for general principles of neural organization for intelligence and try to make intelligent systems out of simplified neurons.

3. Human intelligence is also studied on the psychological level, e.g., with experiments in which human subjects solve problems.

4. Expert system technology is based on the fact that much expert practice is based on large numbers of rules-of-thumb—"*if you see this do that*". Thus Mycin proposes a diagnosis and recommends a treatment for a bacterial infection of the blood on the basis of symptoms and the results of

tests. It knows nothing of bacteria as organisms that grow and reproduce and sometimes emit toxins. In fact Mycin knows nothing of processes occurring in time. It is not evident how general knowledge about events in general and bacteria in particular could be used in a Mycin-like program. Expert system technology has turned out to be useful for carefully selected (or just fortunately selected) problems. Some enthusiasts believe that human level intelligence is just a matter of having enough rules of thumb. Fetzer writes that the problem of expert systems is choosing the right expert. That's rarely the problem because expert system work almost always concerns areas where the experts agree. The problem is the fundamental limitation of collections of rules-of-thumb.

5. The logicist or formal reasoning approach to AI (I do that) studies the kind of "common sense informatic situation" in which intelligence solves problems. It expresses in mathematical logic facts about what information and actions are available for achieving goals and uses logical inference to decide what to do. Common sense is the center of its domain, and it sees scientific theories, e.g. physics, as embedded in common sense knowledge and reasoning. Its needs have led to formalizing* nonmonotonic reasoning.

6. Contiguous with the logicist approach to AI are philosophical studies of epistemology and theories of mind. These concern what knowledge is, how it is to be obtained and how it is possible for (a human) to know. The many schools of epistemology and philosophy of mind take different views of artificial intelligence. These range from active cooperation in formalizing phenomena of AI interest (e.g., knowledge and causality), through Daniel Dennett's *"intentional stance"* that ascribes mental qualities in a way quite congenial to AI, to total disdain for the possibility of intelligence in non-biological systems. Because mind has always been central to philosophy, philosophical schools have developed opinions about what constitutes knowledge, cause and mind. These opinions have led many philosophers to be boldly prescriptive about what AI researchers can and cannot do or should and should not do. Such prescriptions have been about as influential in AI as they have been in other sciences.

Philosophers also engage in conceptual analysis resulting in distinctions, and sometimes AI researchers find these distinctions useful.

However, sometimes what purports to be merely a conceptual distinction turns out to make empirical claims, and sometimes these claims are false. One series of such inadvertent claims concerned the incorrigibility of reports of pain and was discussed by Daniel Dennett (1978). Another was made by John Searle, who asserted (1990) that a Chinese dialogue could equally well be interpreted as the score of a chess game or stock market predictions by a person unfamiliar with Chinese. This contradicts the experience of cryptography, the decipherment of ancient languages and (most likely) algorithmic information theory.

I bet you thought I'd never get around to talking about the present book.

Fetzer recounts the history of AI research, surveys the fields of AI makes some conceptual distinctions and makes some empirical claims. Although he discusses using logic for representing information, he ignores the logicist approach to AI—thus offending this reviewer.

There is also a considerable difference in emphasis between the AI community and Fetzer's "... the most fascinating question about AI remains whether or not machines can have minds". We would put the question as "What intellectual mechanisms are there, which are required for which tasks, and how can a computer be programmed to implement them?" This difference is already apparent in the foreword, and Fetzer seems unaware that anyone would dissent from the way he structures the issues.

The book covers very many topics related to AI, and I find myself in disagreement in so many places that I'd have to write a whole book to deal with all of them. It's especially hard because I mostly don't like his formulation of the questions rather than merely disagreeing with the answers.

However, there's a main contention, and I'll deal with that. We have on page xiv: "I shall argue that ... digital machines are symbol systems, while humans are semiotic; that only semiotic systems are possessors of minds; and that the prevalent conceptions of AI are based on mistakes."

I take this sentence as asserting that no digital machines are semiotic systems.

When someone asserts that AI cannot do something, there is usually an intuition behind it concerning what computer programs are like, perhaps about how they must represent information. If the person has paid some attention to the AI literature, then the intuition may, more or less, apply to the programs he has read about. Often the intuition can be taken as a challenge, however imprecisely expressed, to extend the capability of AI programs.

Here's an outline of Fetzer's main argument. He introduces a distinction between *symbol* systems and *semiotic* systems. Symbol systems are taken to be what Newell and Simon call physical symbol systems. Next he argues that intelligence requires semiotic systems. He then seems to declare that symbol systems are not semiotic systems. We understand symbol systems, e.g., programs that compute with symbols and also their extensions that generate symbolic expressions from inputs and affect the external world by their outputs. So what are semiotic systems and how are they different?

Semiotic systems involve symbols, the things they denote and the being for whom they denote it. The same symbol can denote different things for different people. When a symbol in a machine denotes something, Fetzer requires that we distinguish between its denoting the thing for the user of the machine and denoting it for the machine itself. I gather he contends the latter doesn't happen and can't happen. An example is that "chair" denotes chairs for Fetzer and me but doesn't really denote chairs *for* the database system of the chair manufacturer.

Fetzer doesn't make the idea more precise, but I would conjecture that he is concerned with this fact that when a person uses "chair" to denote chairs he has another concept of chair to which he relates the word "chair". A pocket calculator may have no other concept of 7 to which it relates the 7-key and the 7-display, although it has an internal representation of numbers which is distinct from these.

I agree that this is a worthwhile distinction, but I think we can make computer programs do it also. It will be important when we make computers introspective in significant ways, i.e., make them use sentences about their own knowledge or lack thereof. Maybe it can be said to happen already in a computer vision or robotic construction program that relates chair to recognition and construction criteria.

On p. 50, Fetzer says

Moreover, there appear to be several unexamined alternatives with respect to Newell and Simon's conception, since other arguments might be advanced to establish that symbol systems properly qualify either as semiotic systems of Type I or Type II or else that special kinds of symbol systems properly qualify as semiotic systems of Type III, which would seem to be an important possibility that has yet to be considered.

By p.52 Fetzer seems to have rejected the possibility, saying;

By combining distinctions between different kinds (or types) of mental activity together with psychological criteria concerning the sorts of capacities distinctive of systems of these different kinds (or types), the semiotic approach provides a powerful combination of (explanatory and predictive) principles, an account that, at least in relation to human and non-human animals, the symbol-system hypothesis cannot begin to rival. From this point of view, the semiotic-system conception, but not the symbol-system conception, appears to qualify as a theory of mind.

I can't find anything between these pages that even purports to supply an argument.

Fetzer (following C.S. Peirce (1839-1914)) puts semiotic systems in three categories—iconic, indicative and symbolic. A statue is iconic, because it looks like the object; a smell of burnt coffee is indicative, because it indicates that someone has left an almost empty coffee pot on the burner; and "chair" is purely symbolic. He points out that Newell and Simon don't treat these iconic and indicative cases in their definition of physical symbol system, and therefore argues that their concept doesn't cover semiotic systems in general. It seems to me that Newell and Simon could easily extend their concept to cover those two cases, because they are even easier to treat then the purely symbolic. It is hard to believe that Fetzer relies so much on what seems to be a quibble.

Fetzer makes another distinction between symbolic and semiotic systems.

Symbolic systems can simulate, i.e., match the i-o behavior of another system whereas semiotic systems replicate, i.e., match the internal behavior as well. This has no obvious relation to the previous distinction.

Moreover, semiotic systems can make mistakes whereas symbolic systems can only malfunction. Distinguishing mistakes from malfunctions is sometimes worthwhile. Indeed any system doing nonmonotonic reasoning can make mistakes, i.e., reach a wrong conclusion because it failed to take into account an important fact. However, nonmonotonic reasoning systems are symbolic.

Another quibble concerns symbols. Newell and Simon use strings of characters as symbols and not the characters themselves. Fetzer seems to think symbols should be elementary.

Finally, let's consider the extent to which AI is ready for Fetzer's implicit challenge to represent the Peircian *semiotic* relation among a symbol, an external object and a person. To deal with persons, we propose to use the notion of formal context now being intensively studied in AI. There isn't yet an exposition of what has been discovered, but (McCarthy, 1987) describes a preliminary approach. R. V. Guha's forthcoming Stanford dissertation will do much more. The idea is to write $ist(c,p)$ to assert that the sentence p is true in the context c. Contexts can be associated with persons in order to handle the third term in the semiotic relation, but they have many other uses.

One basic approach to the formal logic of semiotics involves axiomatizing a term *meaning (term,context)*, where *context* in general involves a person and a situation. In many cases, however, many of the axioms hold in contexts covering many persons and situations. In those (very common) cases, a more conventional meaning theory can be used.

I think AI isn't very far along in meeting the challenge which Fetzer's book partly expresses. Unfortunately, there isn't yet a clear understanding of what the semiotic challenge is, whether from Fetzer or from within the AI community.

With all this, even completely refuting Fetzer's argument that digital machines can't have minds wouldn't constitute much progress. Progress requires consideration of specific mental abilities and how to program the computer to use them.

References:

Dennett, Daniel (1978) "Why You Can't Make a Computer that Feels Pain", in *Brainstorms*, Bradford Books.

McCarthy, John (1987) "Generality in Artificial Intelligence", *Communications of the ACM*. Vol. 30, No. 12, pp. 1030-1035. Also in *ACM Turing Award Lectures, The First Twenty Years*, ACM Press, 1987.

Searle, John (1990) "Is the Brain's Mind a Computer Program? (Artificial Intelligence: a Debate)", *Scientific American*. Vol. 262, No. 1:26, 1990.

13

Review of *What Computers Still Can't Do*

13.1   Progress in Logic-Based AI

Hubert Dreyfus claims that "symbolic AI" is a "degenerating research program", i.e. is not making progress. It's hard to see how he would know, since he makes no claim to have read much of the recent literature.

In defending "symbolic AI", I shall concentrate on just one part of symbolic AI—the logic-based approach. It was first proposed in McCarthy, 1959, attracted only intermittent following at first, but has had an increasing number of workers since 1970.[1] I think other approaches to AI will also eventually succeed, perhaps even connectionism. To contradict an earlier Dreyfus metaphor "AI at the Crossroads Again", it isn't a crossroads but a race including logic based AI, SOAR, connectionism and several other contenders.

How goes the logic-based runner? In fits and starts, as problems are identified and progress made.

Within logic-based AI, I shall emphasize one development—formalized nonmonotonic reasoning, because it illustrates intermittent but definite progress. It was first proposed in McCarthy, 1977, gained momentum with the 1980 special issue of *Artificial Intelligence*, and summarized in the collection Ginsberg, 1987. It has continued to develop, see e.g. Lifschitz, 1993.

---

[1]The logic-based approach doesn't include Newell's Newell, 1992 approach based on Soar, which is also "symbolic AI". A reasonable interpretation of logic-based AI is that it works directly at what Newell, Newell, 1982 and Newell, 1992, calls the logic level.

Minsky (Minsky 1975) mentioned the need for something like non-monotonic reasoning, but used this fact as evidence for the inadequacy of logic-based approaches to AI and the need for approaches not based on logic. This isn't how things have gone. Nonmonotonic reasoning has developed as a branch of mathematical logic, using the concepts, such as that of interpretation and model, that logicians have been developing since the 1930s.

The circumscription method of nonmonotonic reasoning would have been entirely comprehensible to Hilbert and probably even to Frege. However, no formalized nonmonotonic logic was developed until the 1970s. This is typical of the slow progress in developing mathematical logical formalisms. Just consider the sequence, Aristotle, Leibniz, Boole, Frege, Hilbert, Gödel. Each step would have been comprehensible to the predecessor, yet it took a long time for the new ideas to appear. Formalized nonmonotonic reasoning is surely not the last step in the chain aimed at formalizing useful reasoning. Formalizing nonmonotonic reasoning required realizing that there is proper reasoning that is not conclusive and that is often not the same as probabilistic reasoning.

For this reason, neither Dreyfus or anyone else is entitled to conclude that if the logic oriented AI problem hasn't been solved in 40 years, it won't ever be solved. To do that it would be necessary to prove a theorem about limitations of logic. Not even showing that there has been no progress at all would be conclusive. However, Dreyfus makes no reference to nonmonotonic reasoning in his book. That's about 1,000 papers he doesn't know about. However, in answer to a question at a book-selling talk, he said that claiming progress in nonmonotonic reasoning is progress towards AI is like claiming that climbing a tree is progress towards reaching the moon—thus recycling a metaphor from the book.

Although formalized nonmonotonic reasoning was discovered in connection with AI, many logicians pursue it as a purely mathematical study, independent of applications to AI or logic programming (another non-entry in Dreyfus's index).

13.2   The Future of Logic Based AI

The review editors asked me to say what I think the obstacles are to human-level AI by the logic route and why I think they can be overcome. If anyone could make a complete list of the obstacles, this would be a major step towards overcoming them. What I can actually do is much more tentative.

Workers in logic-based AI hope to reach human-level in a logic based system. Such a system would, as proposed in McCarthy, 1959, represent what it knew about the world in general, about the particular situation and about its goals by sentences in logic. Other data structures, e.g. for representing pictures, would be present together with programs for creating them, manipulating them and for getting sentences for describing them. The program would perform actions that it inferred were appropriate for achieving its goals.

Logic-based AI is the most ambitious approach to AI, because it proposes to understand the common sense world well enough to express what is required for successful action in formulas. Other approaches to AI do not require this. Anything based on neural nets, for example, hopes that a net can be made to learn human-level capability without the people who design the original net knowing much about the world in which their creation learns. Maybe this will work, but then they may have an intelligent machine and still not understand how it works. This prospect seems to appeal to some people.

Common sense knowledge and reasoning is at the core of AI, because a human or an intelligent machine always starts from a situation in which the information available to it has a common sense character. Mathematical models of the traditional kind are imbedded in common sense. This was not obvious, and many scientists supposed that the development of mathematical theories would obviate the need for common sense terminology in scientific work. Here are two quotations that express this attitude.

> One service mathematics has rendered to the human race. It has put common sense back where it belongs, on the topmost shelf next to the dusty canister labelled 'discarded nonsense'. —*E. T. Bell*

All philosophers, of every school, imagine that causation is one of the fundamental axioms or postulates of science, yet, oddly enough, in advanced sciences such as gravitational astronomy, the word 'cause' never occurs ... The law of causality, I believe, like much that passes muster among philosophers, is a relic of a bygone age, surviving, like the monarchy, only because it is erroneously supposed to do no harm ... /.—B. Russell, "On the Notion of Cause", *Proceedings of the Aristotelian Society*, 13 (1913), pp. 1–26.

The "Nemesis" theory of the mass extinctions holds that our sun has a companion star that every 13 million years comes close enough to disrupt the Oort cloud of comets, some of which then come into the inner solar system and bombard the earth causing extinctions. The Nemesis theory involves gravitational astronomy, but it doesn't propose a precise orbit for the star Nemesis and still less proposes orbits for the comets in the Oort cloud. Therefore, the theory is formulated in terms of the common sense notion of causality.

It was natural for Russell and Bell to be pleased that mathematical laws were available for certain phenomena that had previously been treated only informally. However, they were interested in a hypothetical information situation in which the scientist has a full knowledge of an initial configuration, e.g. in celestial mechanics, and needs to predict the future. It is only when people began to work on AI that it became clear that general intelligence requires machines that can handle the common sense information situation in which concepts like "causes" are appropriate. Even after that it took 20 years before it was apparent that nonmonotonic reasoning could be and had to be formalized.

Making a logic-based human-level program requires enough progress on at least the following problems:

extensions of mathematical logic Besides nonmonotonic reasoning, other problems in the logic of AI are beginning to take a definite form including formalization of contexts as objects. This can provide a logical way of matching the human ability to use language in different ways depending on context. McCarthy, 1987, Guha, 1991, McCarthy, 1993, Buvac and Mason, 1993.

elaboration tolerance Formalisms need to be elaboratable without a human having to start the formalism over from the beginning. There are ideas but no articles as yet.

concurrent events Gelfond, Lifschitz and Rabinov, 1991 treats this using the situation calculus, and I have some recent and still unpublished results aimed at a simpler treatment.

intentionality The treatment of mental objects such as beliefs (much discussed in the philsophical literature) and the corresponding term concept, e.g. "what he thinks electrons are" (hardly at all discussed in the formal literature).

reification We need a better understanding of what are to be considered objects in the logic. For example, a full treatment of the missionaries-and-cannibals problem together with reasonable elaborations must allow us to say, "There are just two things wrong with the boat."

introspection and transcendence Human intelligence has the ability to survey, in some sense, the whole of its activity, and to consider any assumption, however built-in, as subject to question. Humans aren't really very good at this, and it is only needed for some very high level problems. Nevertheless, we want it, and there are some ideas about how to get it. What may work is to use the context mechanism as discussed in McCarthy, 1993 to go beyond the outermost context considered so far.

Unfortunately, too many people concentrated on self-referential sentences. It's a cute subject, but not relevant to human introspection or to the kinds of introspection we will have to make computers do.

levels of description If one is asked how an event occurred, one can often answer by giving a sequence of lower level events that answer the question for the particular occurrence. Once I bought some stamps by going to the stamp selling machine in the airport and putting in six dollars, etc. Each of these subevents has a how, but I didn't plan them, and cannot recall them. A stamp buying coach would have analyzed them to a lower level than I could and would be able to teach me how to buy stamps more effectively. For AI we therefore need a more flexible notion than the computer science theories of how programs are built up from elementary operations.

Dreyfus asks why anyone should believe all this can be done. It seems as good a bet as any other difficult scientific problem. Recently progress has become more rapid, and many people have entered the field of logical AI in the last 15 years. Besides those whose papers I referenced, these include Raymond Reiter, Leora Morgenstern, Donald Perlis, Ernest Davis, Murray Shanahan, David Etherington, Yoav Shoham, Fangzhen Lin, Sarit Kraus, Matthew Ginsberg, Douglas Lenat, R. V. Guha, Hector Levesque, Jack Minker, Tom Costello, Erik Sandewall, Kurt Konolige and many others. There aren't just a few "die-hards".

However, reaching human level AI is not a problem that is within engineering range of solution. Very likely, fundamental scientific discoveries are still to come.

13.3   Common Sense in Lenat's Work

Douglas Lenat is one of the few workers in AI at whose recent work Dreyfus has taken a peek.

Dreyfus, p. xvii and xviii, writes:

> When, instead of developing philosophical theories of the transcendental conditions that must hold if the mind is to represent the world, or proposing psychological models of how the storage and retrieval of propositional representations works, researchers in AI actually tried to formulate and organize everyday consensus knowledge, they ran into what has come to be called the commonsense-knowledge problem. There are really at least three problems grouped under this rubric:
>
>   1. How everyday knowledge must be organized so that one can make inferences from it.
>   2. How skills or know-how can be represented as knowing-that.
>   3. How relevant knowledge can be brought to bear in particular situations.
>
> While representationalists have written programs that attempt to deal with each of these problems, there is no generally accepted solution, nor is there a proof that these problems cannot be solved. What

is clear is that all attempts to solve them have run into unexpected difficulties, and this in turn suggests that there may well be in-principle limitations on representationalism. At the very least these difficulties lead us to question why anyone would expect the representationalist project to succeed.

That's not too bad a summary except for the rhetorical question at the end. Why should one expect it to be easy, and why should one expect it not to succeed eventually in reaching human level intelligence? Most of the people who have pursued the approach have seen enough of what they regard as progress to expect eventual success. I have referred to some of this progress in my account of the invention and development of formalized nonmonotonic reasoning.

Mostly I agree with what Lenat said (as Dreyfus quotes him in the book), and I don't find much support for Dreyfus's assertions that empathy rather than just verbalizable understanding is required in order to understand human action. I think the example on p. xix of what "it" means in

Mary saw a dog in the window. She wanted it.

is within the capability of some current parsers that use semantic and pragmatic information.

However, I think the following assertion of Lenat's Lenat and Guha, 1990 quoted by Dreyfus on p. xxv is an oversimplification.

These layers of analogy and metaphor eventually 'bottom out' at physical-*somatic*-primitives: up, down, forward, back, pain, sssss-cold, inside, seeing, sleeping, tasting, growing, containing, moving, making noise, hearing, birth, death, strain, exhaustion, . . .

The contact of humans (and future robots) with the common sense world is on many levels, and our concepts are on many levels. Events that might bottom out *physically*—as informing someone of something may physically bottom out in making a noise—often don't bottom out epistemologically. We may assert that A informed B of something without our being able to describe the act in terms of making noise or typing on a keyboard.

While I don't agree with Lenat's formulation, the success of Cyc doesn't depend on its correctness. Cyc perfectly well can (and indeed does) store information obtained on several levels of organization and used by programs interacting with the world on several levels.

All this doesn't guarantee that Cyc will succeed as a database of common sense knowledge. There may be to big a conceptual gap in the AI community's ideas of what are the usefully stored elements of common sense knowledge.

13.4   The Degenerating Research Program

In the first edition of Dreyfus's book there were some challenges to AI. Dreyfus said computers couldn't exhibit "ambiguity tolerance", "fringe consciousness" and "zeroing in". These were left so imprecise that most readers couldn't see any definite problem at all. In the succeeding 30 years Dreyfus has neither made these challenges more precise nor proposed any new challenges, however imprecise. It's a pity, because AI could use a critic saying, "Here's the easiest thing I don't see how you can do". That part of Dreyfus's research program has certainly degenerated.

However, I can give a definite meaning to the phrase "ambiguity tolerance" that may not be too far from Dreyfus's vague idea, and with which formalized nonmonotonic reasoning can deal. The idea is that a concept that may be ambiguous in general is to be taken by default as unambiguous in a particular case unless there is reason to do otherwise.

Here's an example.

Suppose that some knowledge engineer has the job of making an adviser for assistant district attorneys. The prosecutor answers some questions about the facts of the case, and the program suggests asking for indictments for certain crimes. We suppose that attempting to bribe a public official is one of these crimes.

We ask whether the knowledge engineer must have anticipated the following three possible defenses against the charge, i.e. have decided whether the following circumstances still justify an indictment.

1. The defendant's lawyer claims that his client did not know the person he offered money to fix his drunk driving convictions was the commisioner of motor vehicles. His client thought he was just an influential lawyer.

2. The defendant's lawyer claims that while his client may have thought he was bribing the commissioner of motor vehicles, he really wasn't, because the Governor had never properly signed the commission.

3. The defendant put an advertisement in the *Criminal Gazette* offering $5,000 to any public official who would fix his conviction. Must the prosecution exhibit a specific public official the defendant was attempting to bribe in order to get a conviction for "attempting to bribe *a* public official".

There may be further potential ambiguities in the statute. If we demand that the knowledge engineer have resolved all of them before he can write his expert system, we are asking for the impossible. Legislators, lawyers and judges don't see all the ambiguities in advance.

Notice that in most cases of bribing a public official, there was a specific individual, and he really was a public official and this was really known to the defendant. Very likely, the legislators had not thought of any other possibilities. The nonmonotonic reasoning approach to ambiguity tolerance says that by default the statute is unambiguous in a particular case. Indeed this is how the law works. The courts will not invalidate a law because of a general amiguity; it has to be ambiguous in a significant way in the particular case.

Since the expert system writer cannot anticipate all the possible ambiguities, he must make his system *ambiguity tolerant*.

When an ambiguity is actually pointed out to the expert system, it would be best if it advised looking at cases to see which way the statute had been interpreted by judges. I don't know whether to be a useful adviser in statutory criminal law, the expert system would have to have a library of cases and the ability to reason from them.

I have not written logical formulas for *ambiguity tolerance*, i.e. expressing the default that a concept, possibly ambiguous in general, is to be considered unambiguous in particular cases unless there is evidence to the contrary. However, I would be strongly motivated to give it high priority if Dreyfus were to offer to bet money that I can't.

To conclude: Dreyfus has posed various challenges to AI from time to time, but he doesn't seem to make any of them precise. Here is my challenge to Dreyfus, whereby he might rescue his research program from degeneration.

What is the least complex intellectual behavior that you think humans can do and computers can't? It would be nice to have more details than were given in connection with *"ambiguity tolerance"* and *"zeroing in"*.

References:

Buvač, Saša and Mason, Ian A. (1993) "Propositional logic of context", in *Proceedings of the Eleventh National Conference on Artificial Intelligence*, to appear.

Gelfond, M., Lifschitz, V. and A. Rabinov "What Are the Limitations of the Situation Calculus?", in *Automated Reasoning: Essays in Honor of Woody Bledsoe*, Robert S. Boyer, (ed.), Kluwer Academic Publishers, Dordrecht, Boston and London.

Ginsberg, Matthew. *Readings in Non-Monotonic Reasoning.* Los Altos, CA: Morgan Kaufmann.

Guha, R. V. (1991) *Contexts: A Formalization and Some Applications*, Stanford Ph.D. Thesis.

Lenat, Douglas and R. V. Guha (1990) "Building Large Knowledge Based Systems: Representation and Inference in the Cyc Project", Addison-Wesley.

Lifschitz, Vladimir (1993) "Circumscription", in *Handbook of Logic for Artificial Intelligence and Logic Programming*, Vol. 3, Oxford University Press.

McCarthy, John (1959) "Programs with Common Sense", in *Proceedings of the Teddington Conference on the Mechanization of Thought Processes*, Her Majesty's Stationery Office, London.

McCarthy, John (1977) "Epistemological Problems of Artificial Intelligence", in *Proceedings of the Fifth International Joint Conference on Artificial Intelligence*, M.I.T., Cambridge, Mass.

McCarthy, John (1987) "Generality in Artificial Intelligence", *Communications of the ACM*. Vol. 30, No. 12, pp. 1030–1035. Also in *ACM Turing Award Lectures, The First Twenty Years*, ACM Press. Reprinted in McCarthy, 1990.

McCarthy, John (1990) *Formalizing Common Sense*, Ablex, Norwood, New Jersey.

McCarthy, John: "Notes on the Formalization of Context", *Proceedings of the Thirteenth International Joint Conference on Artificial Intelligence*, Los Altos, CA, Morgan-Kaufmann.

Minsky, Marvin: "A Framework for Representing Knowledge", in Winston, Patrick (ed.) *The Psychology of Computer Vision*, pp. 211–277, New York, McGraw-Hill.

Newell, Allen: "The Knowledge Level", *Artificial Intelligence* 18 pp. 87–127.

Newell, Allen (1992) *Unified Theories of Cognition*, Harvard University.

Newell, Allen: "Reflections on the Knowledge Level", *Artificial Intelligence* 59 pp. 31–38.

14

Review of *Before It's Too Late: A Scientist's Case for Nuclear Energy*

If the ultimate fate of nuclear energy in the U.S. were entirely to be determined by the politics of 1988, it would be doomed. The Republican candidates are weakly for it, and the Democrats have all taken positions against it and in support of every kind of obstructionism. However, if nuclear energy is really the best option for humanity over the next several hundred years, it will win. Of course, this wouldn't be inevitable if the U.S. were the only country in the world. It has happened in the past, and one can imagine it happening in the future, that a country will firmly follow a path to ruin, regardless of the information available about alternate paths. Fortunately, there are many countries in the world, and France, Japan and the Soviet Union (in spite of Chernobyl) continue to develop nuclear energy successfully. If they're right, and I think they are, we'll eventually wake up, suffering only a little unnecessary poverty and additional loss of technological leadership.

Bernard Cohen, a physicist specializing in health related radiation problems, presents a carefully argued case. He is strongest in treating the problems of reactor accidents, waste disposal and other radiation hazards. He carefully compares the *loss of life expectancy* (LLE) from nuclear energy with other hazards and finds it small. It is also small compared to the LLE of other methods of energy generation and the LLE being caused by the country being poorer.

15

Petition for Withdrawal of *Computing the Future*: A National Research Council report

Dear Colleagues in Computer Science and Engineering:

We are asking you to join us in asking the Computer Science and Telecommunications Board of the National Research Council to withdraw for revision its report entitled "Computing the Future: A Broader Agenda for Computer Science and Engineering", because we consider it misleading and even harmful as an agenda for future research. Our objections include its defining computer science in terms of a narrow set of applied objectives, and its implication that the tone of computer science is to be set by government agencies, university administrators and industrialists and that computer scientists are just the "soldiers on the ground".

There is much useful information in the report, but the preface and the Executive Summary characterize computer science in a way that no other science would accept. Chapter 2, "Looking to the Future of CS&E", and Chapter 3, "A Core CS&E Research Agenda for the Future" should also not be accepted by computer scientists. The Report merges computer science and computer engineering at the cost of abolishing computer science and seriously narrowing computer engineering.

This was an e-mail message sent to a large number of computer scientists. More than 900 "signed" the e-mail petition urging withdrawal of the report

Besides individual scientists, we hope that some computer science departments will collectively join in requesting the report's withdrawal.

Our campaign for the report's withdrawal is being conducted entirely by electronic mail, and we will be grateful to anyone who forwards this message to others who might be concerned. Email to signatures@cs.stanford.edu will be counted as signing the petition, not as necessarily agreeing to everything in this message. In fact, the sponsors of this message are committed to the petition and not necessarily to every detail of the message. We haven't taken the time to hash out every detail. So "sign" if you endorse the petition sent as a separate message.

This message contains the following parts:

1. The introduction preceding this table of contents.
2. The reasons why the report should be withdrawn.
3. The preface and executive summary of the report itself.
4. Some relevant email addresses.

15.1   Objections to the Report

1. What we most object to is exemplified by TABLE ES.1 of the executive summary and the note following it.

TABLE ES.1 Importance of Core Subfields of CS&E to Selected Applications

Core Subfield	Applications			
	Global Change Research	Computational Biology	Commercial Computing	Electronic Library
Multiple processors	Very important	Central	Important	Very important
Data communications and networking	Central	Important	Central	Central
Software engineering	Important	Very important	Central	Important
Information storage and management	Central	Very important	Very important	Central
Reliability	Very important	Important	Very important	Important
User interfaces	Very important	Very important	Central	Central

NOTE: The core subfields listed in TABLE ES.1 constitute a **future research agenda for CS&E**. As significantly, they are important to, and can derive inspiration and challenging problems from, these selected application domains. The core subfields correspond to areas in which major qualitative and quantitative changes of scale are expected. These areas are processor capabilities and multiple-processor systems, available bandwidth and connectivity for data communications and networking, program size and complexity, management of large volumes of data of diverse types and from diverse sources, and the number of people using computers and networks. Understanding and managing these changes of scale will pose many fundamental problems in CS&E, and using these changes of scale properly will result in more powerful computer systems that will have profound effects on all areas of human endeavor.

[End of excerpt from Executive Summary. The bold face is ours.] This simply doesn't do justice to computer science as a branch of science. No areas of research are mentioned. On page 22 of the body of the report is a quite conventional taxonomy of computer science taken from a paper by Peter Denning. There the subfields are listed as:

> Algorithms and Data structures
>
> Programming language
>
> Computer architecture
>
> Numeric and symbolic computation
>
> Operating systems
>
> Software engineering
>
> Databases and information retrieval
>
> Human-computer interaction

This is not great but is recognizable. However, the Executive Summary does not refer to this classification.

2. Our second objection is exemplified by the list on page viii of

Given the increasing pervasiveness of computer-related technologies in all aspects of society, the committee believes that several key groups will benefit from an assessment of the state of academic CS&E:

- Federal policy makers, who have considerable influence in determining intellectual directions of the field through their control of research budgets and funding levels;

- Academic computer scientists and engineers, who are the "troops on the ground" that do research and teach students;
- University administrators, who play key roles in setting the intellectual tone of the academic environment; and
- Industry, which is by far the major employer of CS&E baccalaureate holders, one of the major employers of CS&E Ph.D. recipients, and (in the computer industry) a key player in CS&E research.

Each of these groups has a different perspective on the intellectual, fiscal, institutional, and cultural influences on the field, and the committee devoted considerable effort to forging a consensus on what should be done in the face of the different intellectual traditions that characterize various subfields of CS&E and of different views on the nature of the problems that the field faces.

The metaphor "troops on the ground" expresses an attitude toward computer scientists. The Report sees the content of computer science as mainly determined by Federal policy makers, university administrators and industry. We "troops on the ground" are perhaps to be asked for suggestions from time to time. No report on the research agenda of mathematics or physics would tolerate university administrators "setting the intellectual tone" of the field. It wouldn't be imagined that university administrators had anything to do with it. The report is likely to encourage a regrettable bossiness in otherwise perfectly reasonable deans.

One could argue that this is just an unfortunate wording that could readily be fixed, but it fits well with the idea that computer science has no independent existence but is determined by the problems of the owners of computers.

3. Another dominant attitude of the report is expressed on page 3 by

"Assumptions of the 1940s and 1950s regarding the positive social utility of basic research (i.e., research without foreseeable application) are being questioned increasingly by the federal government, and justifications for research may well in the future require concrete demonstrations of positive benefit to the nation."

Indeed such tendencies exist, but in the week the report came out, the President of the United States was in Texas drumming up support for the Superconducting Super-collider, the most expensive device for pure research ever to be built. The report is based on a pre-emptive surrender to anti-science tendencies that are only slightly worse now than they have ever been.

15.2 Discussion

These observations aren't arguments as to why the report should be withdrawn but rather thoughts on how we got into this mess and what is needed to develop ideas about what computer science is and how it can be advanced.

Computer scientists have always had practical arguments as to why our research should be supported. This is unlike physics, where for several centuries, the main justification had to be that it improved mankind's understanding of the world. Thus none of the arguments for or against Galileo were concerned with whether his ideas would help the renaissance papacy in its wars. It has always been easy to couch proposals for support of computer science in practical terms. Nevertheless, computer science does have its fundamental problems and subfields. It would have been well had the committee tried to identify them; certainly many of its members have the necessary qualifications.

Here is a try at identifying some of the problems that give computer science its structure. We can consider both history and currrent problems. It is just a sample, and we think the existing committee could do a better job than this of identifying research goals if they weren't diverted from thinking about science. Anyway such a broad committee is needed if the facilities and people requirements for achieving these goals are to be comprehensively treated.

1. Consider the history of *regular expressions*. They were invented by the mathematical logician Stephen Kleene, and their first appearance was in a RAND Corporation report about 1950. In those days RAND supported much basic research. The motivation was to determine what languages could be recognized by finite automata. Kleene presumably already knew that languages requiring that parentheses match could not be recognized by finite automata, so natural language recognition could not have been his objec-

tive. The main application of *regular expressions* today is in string searching, completely unanticipated by Kleene. They were certainly not invented as part of one of the areas in the Report's "Core Research Agenda." If the Report's recommendations were in force today, a proposal to study what languages were recognizable by finite automata would lose out in competition with proposals that more clearly provided "concrete demonstrations of positive benefit to the nation."

2. McCarthy's work on Lisp and his work on time-sharing were both motivated as means of carrying out his research on artificial intelligence.

3. The relation between the facts that determine what an object is and algorithms that compute it has been studied in mathematical logic and in computer science (both in AI and in mathematical theory of computation). It is a permanent core research area of computer science. It can probably be related to all the core research areas listed in the Report, but it will lose out in competition to much narrower topics more immediately related to any of them.

4. What can be known about the world by a system with given opportunities to observe and interact. This is a key area of artificial intelligence—the formalization of common sense.

5. How to express knowledge of the world in databases.

6. What are lower bounds on the number of operations needed to perform various numerical and symbolic computations, e.g. invert a matrix or store and retrieve information in data structures?

7. What are the important data structures and the operations on them.

8. What are the routine parts of a proof of a mathematical fact, e.g. the correspondence of a computer program to its specifications, that can be done routinely by computer, and what are the creative parts that require either human attention or substantial AI.

9. What are the properties of various search strategies.

10. What aspects of algorithms are parallel and what are essentially serial? This has a certain relation to the Report's multi-processors, and undoubtedly someone could make a case for studying parallelism in general on the grounds that it would help design or

use multiprocessors. One could also make a case for studying thermodynamics on the grounds that it is relevant to automobile engines. However, the committees that evaluate a physics proposal will consider its importance for thermodynamics and not directly for automobile engines.

11. Modularity. What are the opportunities for modularity in descriptions of the behavior of very complex systems? This affects both the analysis of existing systems and the synthesis of new ones.

15.3 Experimental Computer Science

Experimental computer science needs to be distinguished from applied computer science.

Some of it involves experimentally learning what algorithms embodying certain data structures or certain heuristics or certain other ideas.

Some of it involves programs that learn.

Note that high quality displays arose in experimental computer science long before workstations were proposed for engineering.

The chess machines have taught us that certain heuristics are necessary to reach human level performance no matter how much computer power there is. They have helped identify intellectual mechanisms, and their present lavish use of computation tells us that there is a lot still unknown about intellectual mechanisms.

The experimental work on automatic and interactive theorem proving tells us still more about what intellectual mechanisms we do and don't yet understand.

Experimental computer science may benefit from special equipment, either special computers or auxiliary equipment. There needs to be a study of what facilities are required. Fortunately, we are unlikely to require equipment as costly as physics does.

15.4 Administrative Matters

To add your name to the signatories of the petition, send email to signatures@cs.stanford.edu. All mail to that address will be counted automatically as supporting the petition.

Comments to the sponsors of the petition should be sent to sponsors@cs.stanford.edu.

Copies of the full report can be obtained from

National Academies Press 2101 Constitution Ave. Washington, D.C. 20148

    1-800-624-6242

The price is $24.95 per copy + $3.00 shipping per order, and people from California and Maryland have to pay sales tax. Quantity discounts exist. Call them about it if you care. Maybe you won't want it for your permanent library, but if we are successful in getting it withdrawn, maybe it will become a rare book.

Comments directly to the Computer Science and Technology Board should go to the Chairman William Wulf, Wulf@virginia.edu. A copy should go to mblument@nas.edu. That's Marjorie Blumenthal who handles the affairs of the Board. The Chairman of the committee that produced the report was Juris Hartmanis, jh@cs.cornell.edu.

16

Review of *Weapons and Hope*

Nuclear war is like cancer. It's very bad, but none of the recipes for prevention inspire confidence. Maybe there are a few actions that will reduce the risk, but mostly one just hopes. At least with cancer there are statistics, but one can't even know the odds of getting into nuclear war or of surviving it.

Freeman Dyson is a well known theoretical physicist. In the forties, he helped found quantum electrodynamics, a theory whose numerical answers agree with experiment to eleven decimals. Dyson has written extensively, sensibly and imaginatively on human expansion into the universe and other futurist topics.

Dyson discusses seven approaches to reducing the danger of nuclear war. He doesn't guarantee any, but he has something new to say. His main goal is that the adherents of the two main tendencies—rearmament and unilateral disarmament—should understand one another. He classifies attitudes into those of *warriors* and of *victims*. His characterizes warriors a valuing coolness, accurate analysis and as fascinated with the tools of war. He has many illustrations from World Wars I and II.

However, his characterization of the ideology of victims, even apart from the tendentiousness of the term, is murky. The only example given is Helen Caldicott, characterized by moral force accompanied by fuzzy numbers. She has always struck me as a kind of warrior.

An important merit is his emphasis on irreducible uncertainties. We can't know how much of our society could survive nuclear war. We can't know how effective various weapons would be.

The seven strategies are:

Unilateral disarmament Dyson was a pacifist until World War II began
in England. He inclines to believe that unilateral disarmament
would be good if everyone were a Gandhi, but reluctantly gives it
up, because nowhere near enough people are.

He thinks the Soviets couldn't occupy us successfully even if we
were disarmed, but he doesn't discuss how a disarmed U.S. might
deal with methods the Soviets have actually used when needed
to get in control of recalcitrant populations—massive forced ex-
changes of population, the taking and killing of large numbers
of hostages and the destruction of villages where resistance was
strong. He also neglects the fact that surrender wouldn't assure
even peace, since communists are just as quarrelsome among themselves as with others. We might finish as expendable cannon fodder
in a nuclear war among communist powers.

Mutually assured destruction (MAD) Peace is to be assured by each
side being able to inflict "unacceptable damage" on the other,
i.e. destroy the other's society. MAD advocates consider defense
capability and ability to destroy the other side's military capability
as irrelevant and even harmful, because destabilizing. MAD has
been a major component of American policy since the 1960s.

MAD appeals to the mathematical game theorist, because it treats
the West and the Soviet Union symmetrically and requires no
analysis of the actual characteristics of either society.

Dyson points out that the Soviets don't accept MAD. Their doctrine
is that if war is inevitable, they will attack the opposing military
capability in order to protect themselves. He considers this more
conventional military attitude to be morally less evil. Our own military men also seem to prefer counterforce, and our actual posture
has always included some counterforce capability.

Nuclear war fighting This is the view that nuclear war is like other
war only worse. If one has to fight, one strives to knock out the
enemy armed forces, minimize damage to one's own forces and
society and force a surrender. It is the Soviet doctrine. Dyson
points out the enormous uncertainty involved in a major war with

weapons that have never been used. For this reason any doctrine that holds nuclear war to be survivable is unrealistic. However, he doesn't advance the common "peace movement" argument that the doctrine makes nuclear war more likely by encouraging the U.S. leaders to start one.

Emphasizing the uncertainty, Dyson suggest that civil defense measures would be good but can't be counted on. He admires the Swiss nuclear civil defense measures but suggests that they would be unacceptable in the U.S., because if we prepar to survive nuclear war, the Europeans will feel left out.

Limited nuclear war This deals with the Soviet conventional superiority in Europe and the unwillingness of Western Europe to use its greater population and industry to match it. NATO therefore plans to meet a Soviet tank led assault with tactical nuclear weapons. It has been part of Western preparations since the 1950s, but the Soviets have often able to deter preparations by their threat that any use of nuclear weapons would be met by a massive nuclear attack on all their enemies including the U.S. Their ability to make good on this threat has greatly increased in recent years. Dyson considers limited nuclear war unrealistic because of this Soviet doctrine.

Non-nuclear resistance Dyson hopes that conventional weapons, "precision guided munitions" might be developed that would make it possible for us to unilaterally give up nuclear weapons. He ignores the possibility that a further technological developments might restore the advantage to the nuclear side.

Defense unlimited This doctrine would build shelters as the Swiss have done and develop means for shooting down missiles including space-borne and nuclear ABMs. Its opponents claim it is expensive, ineffective and destabilizing. Their worst case scenario is that the Russians suddenly decide that the defense is just about to become so effective that we would be able to destroy them with impunity and therefore attack us. In fact neither we nor they would ever be sure about how effective defensive measures would be, and this would dilute any impulse towards desperate measures. In so far as it turns out to be likely to work at an affordable cost (ten percent of GNP?), it seems like a good option.

Live-and-let-live Dyson ascribes this concept to the late Donald Brennan, who called it "parity plus damage-limiting" and put it in opposition to MAD with the slogan "We prefer live Americans to dead Russians". Dyson summarises it as "We maintain the ability to damage you as badly as you can damage us, but we prefer our own protection to your destruction". He likes it. Put this way, it's the motherhood of concepts. It will be endorsed by the Reagan Administration even with the corollary that in so far as we develop the ability to protect ourselves, we can forego ability to damage the Soviet Union.

Dyson ignores some important questions.

- What is the present military situation? The Reagan defense build-up is based on the opinion that recent years have seen the Soviets acquire a large military advantage and that re-armament is required to avoid tempting them. Is that right? I have no independent opinion, but I think the people, e.g. Edward Teller, who persuasively advocated that position, are thinking about the important question.

- What characteristics of communism are relevant to living in the same world with nuclear-armed communist powers? Dyson doesn't mention communism in his index, and I could find only one peripheral reference to it in the whole book. His chapter on the Russians attributes their aggressiveness and suspicion to their occupation by the Mongols from the 12th through the 16th centuries, a theory he got from his Institute for Advanced Study colleague George Kennan. A Russian exile to whom I mentioned this jeered, "What? Did he forget to mention swaddling clothes"? But then Dyson quotes Kennan approvingly as saying that we pay too much attention to exiles and dissidents.

Since World War II a number of communist powers have appeared, many not under Soviet control. They share its unpleasant characteristics—aggressiveness, secretiveness, suppression of independent opinion, no orderly way of transferring power, economic inefficiency, and a low threshold for committing genocide. It wasn't the Russians who killed a quarter of the population of Cambodia. This suggests that it's not the Mongols, it's communism.

Ignoring such facts leads to error in dealing with the nuclear war problem. For example, Dyson thinks that we missed an opportunity for an agreement with the Russians about nuclear weapons in the late forties that might have established some measure of trust. He doesn't even mention Stalin and deal with the evidence that Stalin never trusted even his fellow communists and always strove to get them under his thumb. Communist doctrine as well as the personal characteristics of the leaders of these dictatorial regimes plays an important role in limiting the agreements that are possible. Most likely we cannot achieve substantial mutual trust with communist countries until their societies evolve into more humane forms. Indeed maybe some of them will evolve into even more aggressive forms. Here Dyson should apply his own doctrine of living with uncertainty.

A final opinion: We have avoided nuclear war for forty years with a wide variety of policies. We should not let anyone stampede us into desperate measures of either military action or unilateral disarmament. Most likely nuclear peace will continue, but we will not soon achieve a world in which we will really feel safe. Dyson's book contributes to the moderation needed to live in this uncertain world.

17

Review of *The Fifth Generation—Artificial Intelligence and Japan's Computer Challenge to the World*

Japan has replaced the Soviet Union as the world's second place industrial power. (Look at the globe and be impressed). However, many people, Japanese included, consider that this success has relied too much on imported science and technology—too much for the respect of the rest of the world, too much for Japanese self-respect, and too much for the technological independence needed for Japan to continue to advance at previous rates. The Fifth Generation computer project is one Japanese attempt to break out of the habit of copying and generate Japan's own share of scientific and technological innovations.

The idea is that the 1990s should see a new generation of computers based on "knowledge information processing" rather than "data processing". "Knowledge information processing" is a vague term that promises important advances in the direction of artificial intelligence but is non-committal about specific performance. Edward Feigenbaum describes this project in *The Fifth Generation—Artificial Intelligence and Japan's Computer Challenge to the World*, predicts substantial success in meeting its goals, and argues that the U.S. will fall behind in computing unless we make a similar coherent effort.

The Fifth Generation Project (ICOT) is the brainchild of Kazuhiro Fuchi of the Japanese government's Electro-Technical Laboratory. ICOT, while supported by industry and government, is an independent institution. Fuchi has borrowed about 40 engineers and computer scientists, all under 35, for periods of three years, from the leading Japanese computer companies. Thus the organization and management of the project is as innovative as one could ask. With only 40 people, the project is so far a tiny part of the total Japanese computer effort, but it is scheduled to grow in subsequent phases.

The project is planned to take about 10 years, during which time participants will design computers based on "logic programming", an invention of Alain Colmerauer of the University of Marseilles in France and Robert Kowalski of Imperial College in London, and implemented in a computer programming language called Prolog. They want to use additional ideas of "dataflow" developed at M.I.T. and to make machines consisting of many procesors working in parallel. Some Japanese university scientists consider that the project still has too much tendency to look to the West for scientific ideas.

Making parallel machines based on logic programming is a straight-forward engineering task, and there is little doubt that this part of the project will succeed. The grander goal of shifting the center of gravity of computer use to the intelligent processing of knowledge is more doubtful as a 10 year effort. The level of intelligence to be achieved is ill-defined. The applications are also ill-defined. Some of the goals, such as common sense knowledge and reasoning ability, require fundamental scientific discoveries that cannot be scheduled in advance.

My own scientific field is making computer programs with common sense, and when I visited ICOT, I asked who was working on the problem. It was disappointing to learn that the answer was"no one". This is a subject to which the Japanese have made few contributions, and it probably isn't suited to people borrowed from computer companies for three years. Therefore, one can't be optimistic that this important part of the project goals will be achieved in the time set.

The Fifth Generation Project was announced at a time when the Western industrial countries were ready for another bout of viewing with alarm; the journalists have tired of the "energy crisis"—not that it has been solved. Even apart from the recession, industrial productivity has stagnated; it has actually declined in industries heavily affected by environmental and safety innovations. Meanwhile Japan has taken the lead in automobile production and in some other industries.

At the same time, artificial intelligence research was getting a new round of publicity that seems to go in a seven-year cycle. For a while every editor wants a story on Artificial Intelligence and the free lancers oblige, and then suddenly the editors get tired of it. This round of publicity has more new facts behind it than before, because expert systems are beginning to achieve practical results, i.e. results that companies will pay money for.

Therefore, the Fifth Generation Project has received enormous publicity, and Western computer scientists have taken it as an occasion for spurring on their colleagues and their governments. Apocalyptic language is used that suggests that there is a battle to the death—only one computer industry can survive, theirs or ours. Either we solve all the problems of artificial intelligence right away or they walk all over us.

Edward Feigenbaum is the leader of one of the major groups that has pioneered expert systems—with programs applicable to chemistry and medicine. He is also one of the American computer scientists with extensive Japanese contacts and extensive interaction with the Fifth Generation Project.

Pamela McCorduck is a science writer with a previous book, *Machines Who Think*, about the history of artificial intelligence research.

The Fifth Generation contains much interesting description of the Japanese project and American work in related areas. However, Feigenbaum and McCorduck concentrate on two main points. First, knowledge engineering will dominate computing by the 1990s. Second, America is in deep trouble if we don't organize a systematic effort to compete with the Japanese in this area.

While knowledge engineering will increase in importance, many of its goals will require fundamental scientific advances that cannot be scheduled to a fixed time frame. Unfortunately, even in the United States and Britain, the hope of quick applications has lured too many students away from basic research. Moreover, our industrial system has serious weaknesses, some of which the Japanese have avoided. For example, if we were to match their 40 engineer project according to output of our educational system, our project would have 20 engineers and 20 lawyers.

The authors are properly cautious about what kind of an American project is called for. It simply cannot be an Apollo-style project, because that depended on having a rather precise plan in the beginning that could see all the way to the end and did not depend on new scientific discoveries. Activities that were part of the plan were pushed, and everything that was not part of it was ruthlessly trimmed. This would be disastrous when it is impossible to predict what research will be relevant to the goal.

Moreover, if it is correct that good new ideas are more likely to be decisive in this field at this time than systematic work on existing ideas, we will make the most progress if there is money to support unsolicited proposals. The researcher should propose goals and the funders should decide how he and his project compare with the competition.

A unified government-initiated plan imposed on industry has great potential for disaster. The group with the best political skills might get their ideas adopted. We should remember that present day integrated circuits are based on an approach rejected for government support in 1960. Until recently, the federal government has provided virtually the only source of funding for basic research in computer technology. However, the establishment of industry-supported basic research through consortia like the Microelectronics and Computer Technology Corporation (MCC), set up in Austin, Texas under the leadership of Admiral Bobby Inman, represents a welcome trend—one that enhances the chances of making the innovations required.

18

Review of *Not in our Genes: Biology, Ideology and Human Nature*

Scientific study of the contributions of heredity and environment to human abilities and behavior began with Francis Galton in the 1860s. He studied "hereditary genius", concluded that heredity was more important than environment and initiated the eugenic movement to improve humanity. Eugenics had the positive goal of encouraging more children among people with good heredity and the negative goal of preventing reproduction of bad heredity, especially the feeble-minded. Its influence peaked in the 1920s and then fell off for several reasons. Some of its supporters built in their prejudices into their ideas of what were good genes. Coercive social measures, including sterilization of the institutionalized retarded, came into public disfavor. The Nazis used it as a rationalization for genocide. The left, which had favored eugenics in line with its rationalism, became moved to environmental theories which promised quicker results. They were also disappointed that increased equality of opportunity did not bring about complete equality of result.

Like many other issues, the heredity of behavior heated up in the 1960s. Proposers of "affirmative action" to achieve equality of result need the assurance that observed inequalities of accomplishment must be the result of discrimination of some kind, even when overt discrimination has already been eliminated. Since the 60s, scientists whose studies support the view that important components of human behavior are hereditary have been attacked—some to the extent of having their lectures disrupted.

Lewontin and Kamin are two leaders of American "radical science" aka critical science, and Rose is similarly active in Britain. Lewontin has a substantial scientific reputation in evolutionary genetics. Their book bills itself as an answer to the

> New Right ideology . . . with its emphasis on the priority of the individual over the collective. That priority is seen as having both a moral aspect, in which the rights of individuals have absolute priority over the rights of the collectivity—as, for example, the right to destroy forests by clear-cutting in order to maximize immediate profit—and an ontological aspect, where the collectivity is nothing more than the sum of the individuals that make it up.

The authors often bow to Marxism and refer to the bourgeois origin of various concepts. Thus on page 3 they say

> We should make it clear that we use the term *ideology* here and throughout this book with a precise meaning. Ideologies are the ruling ideas of a particular society at a particular time. They are ideas that express the "naturalness" of any existing social order and help maintain it.

However, full-blooded Marxism associates an ideology with each "class" defined by its "relation to the means of production", and explicitly postulates "working class ideology". There is no trace of the proletariat in this book, so we have a kind of attenuated and perhaps less virulent Marxism. Why modern Marxists ignore the "working class" is too complicated for this review. However, it seems to be mutual.

The book accuses those who hold that intelligence, criminality and other human behavioral characteristics have important hereditary components of "reductionism" and "determinism".

Reductionism, they say, is the view that the properties of a complex object are the properties of its parts. Their strawman is the idea that a society is "aggressive" if the individuals that compose it are aggressive. This kind of reductionism fails if the properties of the entity depend on the interaction of its parts. They fail to distinguish between a universal doctrine of reductionism, which I'll bet no one holds, and specific reductionist hypotheses. For example, we believe that the color of an object is not determined by the "colors" of its atoms, but is usually determined by its surface molecules—compounds of small numbers of atoms. Its visual texture, however, is not determined by its molecules but by a larger scale structure. Thus specific reductionist hypotheses may be true or false. When they are true they represent important simplifications, and therefore are often proposed early. The theory that aggressiveness of societies is simply related to the aggressiveness of its individuals cannot be confirmed or refuted solely by general considerations.

This use of the term reductionism is somewhat non-standard. Many people use it to mean that the properties of a complex aggregate is determined by the laws of interaction of its elementary parts, where these laws often take the form of giving the forces between pairs of the elementary parts. Theories of this kind have far greater scope; most present physics takes this form. Such reductionism has opponents called holists, who hold that many important systems, e.g. living beings, are not determined by the elementary interactions of their parts. The holists have so far not been successful in establishing laws that cannot be reduced. The general controversy has turned out to be rather sterile; actual scientific discoveries don't seem to depend on what view a scientist takes of the reductionist-holist controversy.

Determinism, as they use it, seems to require an adjective, e.g. genetic or environmental, to make it definite. Then it is the hypothesis that some properties of an object, e.g. the intelligence of a person, are entirely or mainly determined by one thing, e.g. heredity. Again specific determistic hypotheses are simple, and some of them turn out to be true.

The authors cite many determinist and reductionist hypotheses with which they disagree. These include hereditary determination of IQ, the theory that IQ determines success in academic study, and theories of the biological determination of sex differences in human behavior. One is suspicious of the accuracy with which they cite the views of the people they attack. Perhaps many of them admit more interaction than is ascribed to them.

When attacking a theory such as the one that IQ is about 80 percent hereditary, they demand very high standards of proof. For example, they find all the studies of separated twins to be flawed. (This is apart the fictitious studies of Cyril Burt that Kamin played an important role in exposing).

There is one determinist hypothesis which they accept without applying strict criteria, and that is the hypothesis that their opponents hold their views because they support capitalist society or the oppression of women etc. No criteria are given that would have to be met in order to warrant a conclusion of why someone holds certain views. *In my opinion, a hypothesis about why someone holds certain views requires just as precise a statement and just as convincing evidence as a biological hypothesis.*

The book had considerable critical success. All eleven reviews the Stanford librarians found for me were substantially favorable. (It helped that no less than three of the reviewers were among the fifteen people whose help was acknowledged in the preface as participants in the Dialectics of Biology Group and the Campaign Against Racism, IQ and the Class Society). The reviewers took on the role of a cheering section, applauding blows against the enemy, rather than discussing the plausibility of the positions taken. In this they were somewhat less rational than the authors.

The genetics of human behavior is a difficult scientific subject, and we laymen cannot hope to play an influential role in solving its problems. There are two issues that concern us and that we can influence.

First if scientists are to serve as our representatives in discovering the truth about some important aspect of the world, then we must prevent ideologies from limiting the hypotheses they can consider. Such intimidation reached its extreme in the late 40s when Lysenko with Stalin's help succeeded in destroying Soviet genetics by getting his opponents fired and sending some of them to die in the Gulag. Even the American academic campaign of intimidation which this book serves, has probably succeeded in keeping many young scientists who don't want to be thought reactionary from studying certain hypotheses for fear of liberal disapproval. Thus no one mentions the grimmest hypothesis about the cause of the decline of college entrance examination scores in recent years. Maybe the eugenicists was right and the lower fertility of educated people for 100 years did reduce the number of young people capable of high college entrance examination scores.

The second proper concern of laymen arises when controversies among scientists impinge on public policy. Then we cannot avoid choosing among the rival proposals. However, even without detailed scientific study, we can tell when intimidation is being attempted.

As a computer scientist concerned with artificial intelligence, e.g. making computer programs solve difficult problems, I offer one comment out of my own speciality. Computers differ only in speed and memory capacity; what one can do, another can also be programmed to do—perhaps more slowly. Human non-intellectual capacities vary by factors of two or three; one man can train to lift twice or three times the weight of another. Therefore, if intelligence were like strength, we would expect that an ordinary person could learn to do physics like Einstein or chess like Fischer, only taking several times as long for the same result. Since this obviously doesn't happen, the qualitatively superior intellectual performance of some people over others constitutes a puzzle for the future to solve. Solving it will require an open mind.

19

Review of *The Cult of Information*

It's natural that computers should be surrounded by hype—computers being the symbol of our information age. Bah, I'm beginning to sound like Roszak and the rest of them. Start over.

Computers are important, but there's a lot of exaggeration, and Roszak has found plenty to complain about. However, he exaggerates the dangers and expresses his prejudices. We Earthmen have learned to live with advertisements, and while they sometimes succeed in getting people to spend money in ways I regard as foolish, I never met anyone or even read in the newspapers about anyone who really expects a promotion from using the right soap.

Here are some of the exaggerations Roszak found and some of his own. Here also is my estimate of the phenomena he discusses and some of the issues he raises.

By the way there are also a lot of ordinary inaccuracies, e.g. about when IBM got into the computer business, how the ARPAnet got started, what the phrase "Information please" meant, who are Roger Schank, I.J. Good, Pamela McCorduck and Robert Jastrow, when computer courses began in the universities, what the initials DARPA stand for and whether the New York Times of January 13, 1985 has a page A1. These errors aren't essential to Roszak's arguments, but they arouse doubt.

The cult of information:

Roszak cites assertions that this is the "information age", that our economy is or soon will be based more on information than on goods. Implausible. Ask yourself what you would do with another $20,000 to spend. What fraction would go for information and what for home improvements, cars, travel, eating in restaurants, liquor, dope and supporting orphans in the Third World.

He quotes John Naisbitt's "Megatrends" saying "The new power is not money in the hands of the few, but information in the hands of the many". Nonsense indeed, but it's hard to believe that people will buy more information than they want. Look at the collapse of the home computer boom.

Personal computing:

Roszak finds most of the proposed uses of personal computers not worth the trouble and expense. It's partly true.

I have had a computer terminal in my office and at home connected to the same computer since 1971. I use it for all my writing, for electronic mail and for some programming—I'm a computer scientist. As for information services, we have an Associated Press news wire coming into our computer, I have used the Stanford University on-line catalog and various databases available through dialog. Most people probably wouldn't find this combination of uses sufficient to justify buying a computer or maybe even for maintaining enough expertise to keep using the services. We tried paying bills by computer, but it didn't work too well. Nice but not revolutionary; I'd give up my TV to keep it but not my car. As long as only the present services are available, personal computing will remain a hobby except for people who do a lot of writing, use spreadsheets, or have some other professional reason to compute.

However, I believe that most people will become computer users when the full information resources of our society become available. Here are some examples. To find out what stores carry a desired item at any time of day or night by connecting to its on-line catalog. To be able to read any book or magazine in the Library of Congress, not just its catalog. To send electronic mail to anyone in the world. To be able to comment on any article you read in a way that permits any other reader of the article to summon up any comments that have been made including yours. It still may not be as revolutionary as the car or telephone.

Computer literacy:

Roszak doesn't think much of it, but this is entangled with his idea that it will teach people to think in an algorithmic way which will distract them from "master ideas". His fears are unwarranted. Learning to think in one way doesn't prevent people from thinking in other ways also, and he offers no evidence that teaching computer literacy has had the effects he fears.

Many of the proposals for computer literacy are indeed intellectually deficient. Some proponents say that computer literacy involves overcoming people's fear of computers by letting them sit in front of a terminal, log in, edit files and print papers. This is useful, but it doesn't amount to much intellectually or take much time. The only people I've met who had any real fear of using computers were executives and other big shots. They feared their underlings would get to laugh at their mistakes. The secretaries in our lab were using terminals for word-processing in 1971 and none ever failed to master it, even temporaries, some of whom had never heard of typing into a computer before.

Education in computers should emphasize intellectual value, not immediate practical uses which are readily picked up.

It must include learning to program. It is an individual intellectual breakthrough for each person to discover that it is possible to decide what you want the computer to do and write it down sufficiently precisely that this dumb machine will actually do it. Just controlling an editor isn't enough to really give the idea. Another way of looking at it is this: programming is how we humans talk to our mechanical servants.

What languages should we use? If the teachers could cram it all in, they should learn several languages. An actual machine language tells you what these beasts are really like. A sequential language like BASIC or FORTRAN tells you what most programming is really like. LOGO or LISP tells you how to compute with symbolic information and not just numbers. Finally, logic programming in Prolog lets you express at least some of what you want to tell the computer in the form of facts. Very smart high school students can learn all this in a semester, but most can't. Rather than drag it out, less should be done. If it has to be just one thing, I'd pick logic programming as being closer to how we'll speak to the servants in the future.

While I'm at it I'll express the opinion that the de-emphasis of Euclidean geometry in high school education in favor the pedantic "new mathematics" was a blunder. There are no intellectual surprises in new mathematics, and the student is rightly ungrateful for being reminded of the obvious at tedious length. I remember that my high school geometry book had a proof of Pythagoras's theorem attributed to President Garfield. Here we have an individual whose talents ran to law and politics, not mathematics, and yet the intellectual interest of the subject drew him to finding a new, and somewhat surprising proof, of a 2000 year old theorem.

Roszak doesn't mention one important bad effect computers have had on education, especially at the lower levels. I think teachers aren't as smart as they were when I went to school, and the reason is that too many of the granddaughters of the smart women who taught me are computer programmers. They make better money, and the work isn't as demanding. Something can be done to make entry into teaching easier, e.g. by eliminating required courses in education, but the great expansion of opportunities for intellectual work means that we must learn to do more education with fewer highly qualified people.

Computing and the "true art of thinking":

I'm the computer scientist Roszak cites who said it will take from five to 500 years to reach human level artificial intelligence. There are fundamental conceptual problems to be solved that haven't been properly identified yet. Maybe some clerk in the Swiss patent office has just solved them and hasn't yet published his paper. Maybe they won't be solved for centuries. There is no reason to suppose that reaching human level artificial intelligence is an easier problem than figuring out human heredity, and it took a hundred years to go from Mendel's results with peas to cracking the genetic code. On the other hand the world's leading nuclear physicist, Ernest Rutherford, said in 1937 that there was no hope of nuclear energy, and two years later nuclear fission was properly identified as having actually been observed in 1934. You just can't tell.

Anyway when Roszak quotes a "dean of computer science at Northeastern University" as saying becoming computer literate "is a chance to spend your life working with devices smarter than you are, and yet have control over them. It's like carrying a six-gun on the old frontier", he has indeed found a fool. All present computer programs are extremely specialized and not very smart by human standards. They have no general knowledge of the common sense world, and they can't even accept such knowledge from people.

However, Roszak goes on to say that machine computation is intrinsically different from human thought. This amounts to saying that humans can never understand human thought well enough to make a machine do it. That is a proposition that also requires proof.

The present scientific situation in artificial intelligence is roughly like this. A number of important intellectual mechanisms have been identified and understood well enough to embody them in computer programs. Others are identified but not understood. What we now understand is the basis of an expert system technology that has practical importance. How much practical importance is question that a lot of people are betting a lot of money to find out. While some computer scientists pursue applications, others continue basic research. Recent discoveries assure us that progress continues.

Prejudices:

Running through the book is the theme of establishment plot as in "What computer enthusiasts overlook is the fact that data glut is no some unforseen, accidental fluctuation of supply, like a bumper crop of wheat. It is a strategy of social control, deliberately and often expertly wielded. It is one of the main ways in which modern government and interest groups obfuscate issues to their own advantage".

Also like many academic humanists, he confuses his taste with virtue.

Some of us just appreciate technology the way others appreciate opera. We read about and buy new cameras, hi-fis and computer programs beyond immediate needs the way others buy books. Many also buy books and go to operas.

Contents

IV. The Legislature and the Lord Above

V. Give Everything Away

I. Never Saw the Sea

A woman in Dior

a woman in Dior
lifts a speckled gourd
from a basket on the table

and turns it in the candlelight
even on the vine a gourd looks
dead I always think of them

as magical they have no
television show no aisle
in the bookstore when

I almost drowned I waved
one arm the other
clung to a hunk of ship

at first I could only take
a little water the wine I wished for
all those days made me retch

survivors bend
down to the sand
like giant trees

it's hard for them
to leave things as they are
the town looks strangely

like a field of violets drunk
boys strutting their stems
in shiny jeans for months

I went around smelling of mothballs
I was a knight in rusty clothes
my own beloved

enemy I rode on empty
plains I could not name
the source of anything

the snapper sleeping
on its bed of greens
the lemon necklace

or silver watch the silk
scarf around my neck
I was a woman in Dior

and made obnoxious
toasts and detected in the
wine a hint of cherry

I clapped the waiter
over to please clear away
this pile of bodies

Solomon's Wisdom

Solomon's wisdom didn't keep
him from pining for
sleek horses, so how am I—
with no direct warnings from above—

to keep my mind off you in the bar
mirror fifteen years ago, ice
pouring from the sky behind you, back
when we still believed in winter,

in benevolent bartenders and Peter Buck,
believed no harm could come to us
from drinking Bass with Bushmills
and watching hipsters flaunt

fake fur and silver
by the orange space heaters
until we were thrown out
into a frozen park,

where the glassy trees
reminded us of us—
wrapped brightly
in their misery.

A blade of geese

a blade of geese
defeated any aircraft

until the day a fighter from Chanute
flew so low over us it bent

back shingles on the garage
where my teenaged neighbor

lifted her shirt in front
of me and Toby Gladney

for a dollar her stepfather
was a coke dealer

one night their house lit up
with screaming cops

after two years in Joliet
he came back

quiet and shaven went
around the neighborhood pushing

an old lawnmower
there is no childhood

no girl queen who holds
court in a hollow tree

there is no age to come of
only a pale man

walking in the snow
a shovel on his shoulder

At my mother's house I contemplate my teeth

at my mother's house I contemplate my teeth
consult the televisions about the next hour's weather
splash my face blink away the stars
bless the living room's sick ferns
and walk downtown past the empty Albuquerque Grill
where Joe who used to sweep the sidewalk there
sits on an overturned bucket

he says *how's it hanging*
I tell him it's hanging about the same as usual
that's good he says *when things get unusual*
down there is when you got to worry
I ask him what's going up
where the Burger King used to be
he says *another goddamn Burger King ain't that ironic*
and I wonder if it is in fact ironic
or just vaguely postmodern
or something they do
when the old Burger King fills up with rats
a biplane trails a banner for the Indian casino

construction workers lower PVC
into a trench when the plane flies over
they squint up at the word
the train backs up traffic all the way to Roosevelt
what kind of city can't build a fucking overpass
the faces of the trapped drivers
look sore afraid they crane to read the giant
letters on a chiropractor's billboard
I stand near the tracks and watch prayers
scroll by on black grain cars
there really is no place to go

the train comes to a stop but yellow
stick figures with missing limbs
warn me not to climb between the cars
a couple of new orange tankers lurch
forward like bright Antarctic
mollusks

this is what I do
curse the train curse the goddamn Burger King
wonder about the strange new sea creatures
we've been discovering
when the crossing gates rise people look up from their laps
I see my name on the last car
the slick tracks shaking beneath my feet

First a forest burned

first a forest burned
then grassland

hid the hunters
tonight a silo

squats between two
cities we undress

under a painting
of a muscled

buffalo
car lights flare

between the drawn
curtains steam

creeps under
the bathroom door

I take a beer
from the plastic

ice bucket
and sit on the bed

the clock blinks
fearfully

Like a mendicant

like a mendicant
my father sprawled across a cracked tombstone
his broken glasses at his feet

I cursed the dream cursed his wasted
legs and stubborn chin until Nurse Anne
rolled over and I found the parts

of her I wanted the storm
chaser leaned his impregnable
Toyota into a turn

pulled over on the shoulder
and inspected the cracked windshield
holy shit he said though we

only saw him mouth the words
we circle things Nurse Anne said
like boys on bicycles circle girls' houses

circle each other warily
like cameras
in the underwater

glow of beer commercials
Nurse Anne found the part of me I wanted
to forget the storm chaser

sat in the ditch elbows to knees
and I swear
I saw my father come

swiftly through the field blessing
the short corn stalks
as though he had gone blind

Once I was dangerous

once I was dangerous
I cut my wrists

with red crayon
spied on my high school

neighbor through a warped
fence slat a sheared

sheep rubbed
against her yellow dress

and the gray pipe of her
boyfriend's car

rattled under a chrome
bumper in the cabin

where he had been banished
my father lined up

empties on two-by-fours
nailed in the wall

and every night
my grandmother drove

her knees into the floor
and prayed

until all men grew
headpieces and wings

Uncle Roger roars

Uncle Roger roars
out of April on his beat-up Goldwing
broke and helmetless all the way
to Wakarusa on a gallon

Nurse Anne calls them *donor-cycles*
she doesn't like to flip
the bird at death though I've seen her
torch a Marlboro kitty-corner

from the hospital Uncle Roger
takes a corner under an Indiana sky
blue as the roof of a Long John Silver's
slaps dust from his jeans

puts an arm around my shoulder
and pulls me into the Green Leaf
where the bartender sways
faintly to I Will Dare

as she tips our glasses to the taps
we sit and watch Nurse Anne
through a dusty window
shining in a diesel cloud

like the diamond I once found
in the Vermillion River
I get more beers and Uncle Roger
beams at Nurse Anne's lecture

he persuades the bartender to rig the juke
so it plays for free
we are the only people here and
every second we are getting younger

Among the Machines of Virtue

At the air show sweaty spectators admire the deadly
permutations of Orville Wright's eccentric
dream. I hold myself up

to his example. I blame him for everything.

A Stearman starts to flip and stalls, then turns into the ground
like a kid tripping in a flat

run. The flames remind me of the sun
in Turner's painting. Our mouths

open. Some move toward the blaze
and ring the scene, bowing their heads as if the burning

were an offering for all we have destroyed.

Blackened scraps drift in the sky and fall
like early aircraft—near-miracles dreamed up in the cold
basements of Ohio.

I hold my breath

I hold my breath
driving between the empty auto plant and cemetery

where two maples rise over the gates
like giant lungs the invisible
engine shakes the wheel as the prison's cyclone
fence goes racing by

my cigarette's a minor firework
in the rearview mirror the tailpipe coughing
up black blood

I don't give a fuck

I just adore the crack and hiss of opening
a beer aiming the old four-banger
at the mountainous clouds
looking for another place to wreck

II. Dirty Bomb

Each year gave us portals

each year gave us portals
dark tufts
fought their way

out of the mudhole
a storm washed
gray over

the mountain horses
fled the hillside
the grocery store baker

pulled up smoking
in the funeral-black
back parking lot

some days the ferry
burned he slit huge sacks
of flour with his knife

and poured them
in a big steel mixer
I only have the stomach

for beginnings
the spirit moving
on the face of the waters

the 767 leaning west
a belly full of gasoline
the morning

the firmament dry
land great whale
the word

I step away from the oil fires

I step away from the oil fires
and go out back where Orion's
giant hand hunts in a field
of yellow asphodel water sluices
through a pipe under the grass
like something I am trying
to discover without vodka
without supercolliders or sunlight
streaking through Chagall
without a mother ship
something to be gleaned
from the impossible
infernos of seven stars
the war is over

More and more

more and more
I fight for sleep

I read Milton
or drop a Valium

in a shot of bourbon
but *Lycidas* tends

to kill me quicker
then I snap awake at four a.m.

Google my college
girlfriend and find her

on the steps of an expensive
Chicago townhouse with

her blonde husband who
looks like a low-level Nazi

or Danish prince
I can only console myself

with this fact
scientists predict

blondes will be extinct
in a hundred years

I hate this Googling
it used to be

you could move away
and make old girlfriends

disappear and why
does Google always win

what about all the other
search engines yearning

to be verbs
I refuse to Google you

my nurse I'd rather Yahoo
like we used to

in your attic apartment
our shadows on the wall

like Kurosawa's samurai
but the sleek

and mathematical
beat out the sensual every time

the present always
drags the past into the future

and here's another thing
the blondes aren't dying out

I Googled *blonde extinction*
and found out it's a hoax

blondes in fact
will live forever

Night Birds

Night birds plumbed the aspen grove
below a deck of desperate smokers.
All the houses of the valley gave off tiny suns.

Nurse Anne dressed me in a yellow tie,
linen suit and sandals,
then barreled down the freeway

toward Tinley Park. I don't know what to do
at parties—I pretend I'm Daryl Strawberry,
my pockets stuffed with pills.

When we pulled up to the mansion
I threw three pennies in the fountain
and made my modest wishes:

ten years for a dying father; minor fame;
a sexual fantasy I won't disclose. Hidden
spotlights from the high white

ceiling shimmered on the dresses
of two women dancing. All night
I wondered

what was in a few tightly shut
rooms upstairs. I'm terrible at parties,
I pretend I'm Sherlock Holmes

and rifle every medicine cabinet and drawer,
but I'm sick of discovering
everyone's countless illnesses.

Nurse Anne spent the evening flirting
with a man I swear was Henry Winkler,
his right hand

inching toward her like a pale
wet worm. I stomped out on the deck
to watch the diving birds,

and added the dancing redhead
to my fantasy—hoping a taste of her
own medicine would cure

Nurse Anne's philandering. I never
know what to do in bed.
I do what Nurse Anne says,

asthmatically gasping
under her down comforter.
I hate parties.

I pretend I'm in a children's story,
where any door might lead to paradise
if opened in the proper spirit.

Too good to be police

too good to be police
I sort recycling apologize
for cutting people off always
look a woman in the eye

but some nights I end up on the roof
again drunk as an Exxon Valdez
grasping for Nurse Anne
like a desperate gear

there are no one-way elevators
always rising no leakproof
tankers I only wish my nurse
would lie back with me and listen

to the susurrus of oil
spilling from my hull

Humans are terrible drivers

humans are terrible drivers
terrible sous-chefs and presidents
horrible fathers

I mess with my phone
in my horrible
hybrid feeling smug

I yell at the kids
when I'm pissed
or hungover cursing

each morning's recurring
stubble the spidery
wrinkles and horrible

holes where the musical
instruments and delicate
bellows should be

I'm a terrible teenager
a knife in my locker
my mattress lined with blood

money and porn
horny as ever
I covet my neighbor

her long red boots
jutting from her Honda
as I back from the driveway

breathless and heavily
armed I'm an atrocity
waiting to happen

but she's terrible too
flashing behind an immaculate
window as torturers

tighten the leather
laughing at the one
about the whore

I spend all night online
searching for the perfect
video the silent bloom

of Little Boy over
Hiroshima the latest
dance

I'm looking for dream
homes in missile silos
horribly bored

The Last Romantics

It's not funny anymore. He grunts
like a shaggy bear
when she turns him over in the sun
and ribs him with a playful
finger, or bides her time
plucking out his stiff gray hairs.

The boys he's fending off are slight
and hairless like exotic pets—their skins
are taut as snares. When they dance they dance
on ecstasy and glisten—he has fantasies
of gutting them like clueless salmon.
His books are from another century.

She loves to read to him. She needs
to be on top. She's always running
out for cigarettes. He hasn't smoked in years,
except in dreams he wakes from in a panic. He runs
on treadmills now, takes a yoga class. It's still
a tragedy when she puts on her dress.

I've been destroyed

I've been destroyed
it takes forever to rebuild
one tower

the tunnel closed

noiseless
scraps of skirts drift down
a hurricane of currency

makes it difficult to dream
of a sky beyond the billows

of running in the grass
startling sparrows

Extremist Sonnet

This small world
contains a starfish

pressed on the beach
like a crippled hand,

crumpled baby pictures, the
handsome strangers of the Internet,

and Bin Laden's tiny
television. Pine trees shivering

like addicts on the mountain.
I wanted to tell you about the bees.

I wanted to ask the youth if they are over
being shocking, to say one night

I came home drunk and watched
Daniel Pearl's beheading.

Dirty Bomb

dear sleeper cell
you would adore

this thunder
illumining the scrub

where decapitated pirates
of the drug war hover

the only power
left the only politics

is the river needling
through the canyon

the cave mouths
hanging open

———

dear dirty bomb
there's no riot

like the present
no plot like

a wildfire or desert
crossing

it was never easy
to tell terror

from security
cloud from plume

economic growth
from chemical collapse

———

dear flame
I want to show you

the last downed tree its roots
a reminder of the long

looted cables through which our
art once streamed

I lined the hearth with
bright melted stones

from the crater
went through all the books

nothing but the sacred
left to burn

III. The South

Odds

Then we were at odds,
the sky draped stiffly
over us like a Confederate
uniform hauled up from
the basement for a wedding.

We sat in the green
shape of our suffering,
lilac blossoms blowing,
a distant voice
only the windward heard.

Our child, you said,
and a crooked haircut
came into my mind and his
face: one inexplicable bud
at odds with everything.

After a football game

after a football game
the rollicking stars came out
and shaggy boys sat in the windows
of passing cars as if there'd been a coup

I met up with a woman in a rowdy bar
she was going through a divorce
making sure she did it right
like a stock car going through

a retaining wall
sun-tired and hardly
talking we watched the dancing
students skew the beauty scale

she ran her hands through new
red streaks in her blonde hair
watching highlights on the angled
screen above the bar

our running back
lying face up on the field
a trainer holding both sides of
his helmet like a crystal ball

Three girls

three girls
draw their pretty toes
in the white sand

their wet pink brains
make mine feel

like a gray mothball
as they saunter
over a dune

leaving a shallow groove
in my hangover

Painting

I followed the pillar of smoke
and felt the neighborhood go
from white to black as the faces

of front porches sank
below the hillside
cemetery where they say the dead

are buried standing up. Cop cars
sent garish Morse code into the dark
and a firefighter unspooled

a hose from a yellow tanker
and dragged it toward the house.
The day before

a new show opened at the gallery
downtown, a series of vivid orange
abstracts the owner feared

would never sell. I put up a hand
against the heat. Only a heartless fool
would think of those strange paintings while . . .

I used to see the old woman
tending vegetables in her scraggly yard.
The firefighters retreated into the road like divers

battling a giant eel. An ambulance idled,
going nowhere. The underground
regiments stamped their boots.

The South

There's a giant map on my bedroom wall
where I pin yellow and red tacks
to show the lands I've conquered—the little towns
in Mexico, the grim airport of Dayton, Ohio . . . Geography
has been hard on me. I wanted to live
beneath a mountain, or in New York or London,
to spend time underground, but ended up
instead in Tuscaloosa, Alabama, with only
a dusty closet to hide in during storms.

I learned the efficacy of an artful lie, and sat around
with lolling men in plastic chairs, watching the tomatoes grow,
bickering about such universal subjects
as football and the weather. Smoke poured from the rib joint
like a message and the fat man said,

I keep eating these they'll never fit me in my morgue drawer.

The hickory and grease and vinegar was a miracle
with a sweating can of Miller. Some nights the rain
was warm as bathwater. Blood
crawled in my veins like poisoned roaches. And by God
it didn't matter if your plane was bound
for the domes of Heaven
or the steaming maw of Hell,
you'd be stopping in Atlanta first.

I jump down from my soapbox

I jump down from my soapbox
like Jay Bennett leaping off his Marshall stack
at the Titanic Love Affair show at Treno's pizza,
the one where Matt Pearson went up on stage between sets
and chugged two full pitchers of Leinenkugel,
then lay slumped across a rickety table the rest of the night,
even when Jay turned up his amp so loud
the black walls billowed. The one where Rachel looked
so sullen and amazing in her silver skirt
it took three pints before I got the nerve to yell
something in her ear.

Treno's is long gone. Rachel went and disappeared
into the South. Jay lies dead in his apartment
and I'm back in the Midwest, walking
by the county courthouse on a Sunday,
where the only sign of life is a pair of cardinals
shuddering in a maple like a lunatic's bloodshot eyes.

The sky is a massive hole
over Democratic headquarters and I wonder
who would want to be the mayor of this shitty town.

Better than the undersecretary of some imagined past,

answers my inner enemy, but I don't have to listen
to that voice today. I climb up with the birds
and find Jay perched there
blasting out the riff from "Only in the Past" on his Telecaster,
and Rachel shows up to kiss me hard on the mouth,
for old times' sake we both agree, and Eddie Schaler's dirty van
comes screeching around the corner and when the doors

fly open, Matt, and Ken jump out with Cindy, the drummer
    from Milo,
on whom I had such a terrible crush, and Tim Kauffman in his
    dirty dreads,
and my old girlfriend Monica who gives Rachel that Baltic stare

she used to throw at me sometimes,
and a grinning Eric Appleton,
The Master and the Margarita tucked under his wing.
We're all sitting on branches and someone shouts,

Screw Jeff Tweedy, who cares if he's a genius!

and we all look at Jay and laugh, but he just kills it
like he always did, throwing back his nest of hair.
Nothing's changed since 1992,
and none of us give a damn if we live forever.

Those Who Favor Fire

The way she slid a beer across the bar
made every man a rival,
even legless Gene who climbed
his barstool every night

and told the dirty joke
of his vacation in Khe Sahn,
or marveled at her Great
Dane's massive balls.

My mousehole apartment
was a tent pitched in the
ragged dark I crawled
into for moonless sleeps,

but the Blind Pig's ceiling
shot up like a cathedral
tower—you could let loose
your voice in anger or praise—

it swallowed everything
except her whisper, which always
hushed us like a minister. The two
front windows were the great sow's

eyes through which we saw
the dry cold world
we didn't want. We chose
her brown eyes instead,

glowing in the bottle light.
Some nights turned into
breakfast—the Blind Pig
never seemed to close,

and she never made it
to Montana, as every night
she swore she would. When
her Pontiac skidded off

I-59 we crumpled
napkins in lowballs
and burned them on the bar,
saying nothing.

IV. The Legislature and the Lord Above

I saw you crossing Delaware

I saw you crossing Delaware,
a green scarf flung around your throat,
and hid in the drugstore doorway,
wishing I could drink another beer
and watch the boys watch you
in the bar mirror. You waited at
the intersection tapping your long boots,
then a raft of men bore you through
the polluted air. I went inside for
my prescription, thinking of
General Washington (who had your
serious chin), and of Monroe's inaccurate
stars, crumpling in the misty light
beside the baffled horses.

Heroin chic came back

heroin chic came back
the underage
crouched outside
the bar and picked black
polish from their toes
their feet pale as
fresh concrete the crows
on the crenellated roof
looked dipped in oil
a punk band howled
rattling the windows
of a beat up Civic
the street was full
of foils girls like
tomato stakes
who got their calories
from vodka boys
with bottle caps
jammed in their ears
laughing was how they
bared their teeth at the law
offices across the street

there are so many
kinds of pleasure

The geese had lost their minds

the geese had lost their minds
and spent our awful winters

perched on sunken shopping
carts in Silver Creek

hissing children
from the playground

so the city organized
a hunt

I held a sign
     THESE MONSTERS

ARE LOVELY TO THE LORD
in the other hand

my slingshot
and pouch of stones

I like the feeling of my fist

I like the feeling of my fist
against a plaster wall
but when I heard you kissed
him in a dark part of the museum

Nurse Anne I tried to let it go
happy to remember lying
in your bed a few dead stars
stuck up on the ceiling

but I always keep my fingers crossed
in case the rage comes back
like the horrible cloud
of Uncle Roger's pigeons

last night I went
swiftly through an alley
punching out the glass
garages don't need windows

anyway said my bloody fist
it was nearly morning
when Uncle Roger
took me on the roof

poured me coffee in a metal cup
and tried to tell me something
about love cracking his broomstick
on the coops to make the pigeons fly

Poem for the Government

bless your bombers faint as herons

tearing atmosphere the rapture of

commandos blowing flimsy doors

and green-gray battle stills behind a

drooping flag the sweet shimmering

fear of an enemy dragging himself a-

cross the sand in night vision bless

the rowdy laughter of blacked-out

rooms and doublespeak the boom-

boxes of our valiant interrogators

here the voters whisper we meet

the faces of our lovers underwater

Social Media

Was February but the dogwood budding.
Was Facebook and the reimagining

of friendship, the ferry I was
after and the flood, the family

sprung fully from my skull,
the early dark and roaring

water, the human
underneath the Ferris wheel.

Slow and stately survives

slow and stately survives
the plains fat catfish deliberate
in a cranny of the quarry

and I lie in this police outline
of sweat numbering sins
thrown stones

and crows on the courthouse
gargoyles like the black eyes
of a judge I am led

to the roof of an empty factory
where I await my sentence
this is your prison

says the woman and draws
her knife in an arc
from one horizon to the other

Occupy

Like beads of mercury
skinny boys

swell in the heat. A
purple howl from the girls

goes up when police
cross into the park.

The memes. The fucking
cops. These kids want everything

getting better—their slick phones
stuffed in back pockets like magic

decks, their girlfriends and governments,
even the black-clad, armored officers

advancing lockstep, night
sticks cutting the air.

Tailed by swirling buzzards I descended

Tailed by swirling buzzards I descended
under a sky of cooling steel the geese
guarding the river eyed me like bitter colonels

as I passed the dam and turned downtown
I didn't even stop in at Doc's for a beer
or tarry at the bus stop with the teenaged lovers

I was finally old enough to press
on when there was business to be done I came to
the concrete courthouse sitting on its concrete

stilts like a ponderous gray bug
a Trojan beetle aliens might use
to breach the city and spread my arms

as an officer blessed me with his wand
I rose in an elevator behind a woman in heels
high as justice's sword and a guy with barbed wire

tattooed around his neck oh how sweet
to be unemployable at the yellow counter
I wrote my name three times to make us free

Paul's Tree Care

The short one does the shouting,
holds the rope by the idling pickup,
while the other guy—tall and gaunt
with a lopsided crew cut—straps
spikes to his boots and climbs
the maple like a giant insect, until
he's high above the towering chimney.
That's a big-ass tree, the short guy says,
as he ties a chainsaw to a rope and hauls
it skyward. It's always the quiet one
who climbs the tree, or shimmies
through a crawl space waking snakes,
or crouches in a dank cellar and
waters the face of a hooded prisoner.

The Legislature and the Lord Above

1.

all I need to turn me on
is the Earth's six point five sextillion tons

is the last pink piece of *toro*
glistening on the ocean's
midriff
            the pyrotechnic

sky is breath-
taking it isn't nearly enough I need

the forest ravaged
the burning ice

2.

I gulp a bourbon to forget
my father's knuckles in my back

the lunacy of poverty
mistakes of my twenties and all
their squalling babies

the whiskey makes my downfall sexy

then I can contemplate
my great idea

writing is the opposite of thinking

3.

Duncan MacDougall proved the soul
is a small house sparrow

mine feels like a landfill

full of fucked-up dishwashers
televisions with their eyes shot out
armless dolls and rotted mattresses

so many people died
they had to stop the excavation

every spot on earth an open grave

4.

I'm white as hell
I burn my mail smoke
a jay and bomb the gig

eyeing the college girls
                    Opportunity
bumbling over a tiny patch of Mars

I don't give two shits about
the legislature or the Lord above

my plan is all the gin in town

I need the cops to get me home

5.

sorry to be serious
I'm fed up with this downer music too

scrolling stoned across an unfinished road
cut cornfields stretched out like marshland
in the darkness like
                    childhood?

two weeks in Jersey every year
                              in 1982
we got the new Atari and life was never any better

this was supposed to be a funny poem
like the final act of Michael Richards

6.

I need to interrupt myself
and say a few words to the nation's youth

your hair is ludicrous
                        no one needs
another photo of you drinking from a Solo cup

you may be our only hope

so put down the fucking phone and drive

I've made mistakes myself but Jesus Christ
you're wearing flip-flops in December

your government is killing children in your name

7.

two Jehovah's Witnesses came to talk
about apocalypse
                    my counter-

argument was we've always been seventy-six percent
disaster
            but now I'm not so sure

we haven't knocked the planet off its hinge

let's just say I can't give up Christmas yet
or open the door to every nut with a sacred text

instead I grow exotic
                        facial hair

and invent new apparatuses for getting blitzed

8.

I suspect my Buddhist friend
is only in it for the hippie girls

you don't need a temple

to feel the hollow
points of school shootings
in your chest
                already life is suffering

the blinking teen at the checkout aisle

where particolored magazines foretell
this Western dominance coming to an end

9.

a reporter's trick is flowers
for the dead girl's mother

and keep the camera's gruesome eyeball hidden

call them stories
to keep from becoming wailing
women

there's a novel in me somewhere

this is for David Cornell Dejong
who taught me humility and despair

10.

every pill in the cabinet
went down my gullet

and the triangle in the corner

of every bottle veterans aren't the only ones
traumatized by war

I screamed this insight at the reeling officer

in the anxiety room they denied me every pleasure
covered the antique TV with gauze

until the bombings looked like action paintings

11.

even the secret orchid
of the anus has its odes

bloom of a muzzle flash

the late train always
disappearing
when I turn out the lights

and nuzzle you from bchind
a police action turning into war

a messy democracy for whatever mess this is

12.

I want to turn this garbage into art
to get the fuck off Facebook
and watch the burn barrel burn

to read the Russians and build recycled
sculptures in the park
and precede every tweet with fifteen drafts

I may have seen too many movies
I may have exaggerated certain things

great works of literature I swore I read

V. Give Everything Away

I want the Internet to stop

I want the Internet to stop
the noise the bathroom sink

dripping like an old clock
when my son climbs

in bed and burns
my arm with the hot crown

of his head I want to filter
out these nightly terrors

to sing the proper hymn
or prayer to bear me

up to the top branches
of nineteen seventy-seven

visible to only those
who art in heaven

I want the Internet to simulate
my father smoking Winstons

at the kitchen table or sinking
in his black chair to watch

Jimmy Stewart spill
from his barstool as the blue

shades darken I want to see
that scene a million times to feel

his shaking hand on my back
when I can't sleep

I know what it is to be white

T. G. Wilkinson House
Muncie, Indiana

I know what it is to be white
and empty with sawdust
piles mirrored in the appliances'
dulled luster the old dog
used to drag me up the walk
to piss on your ragged hostas
but the new dog doesn't
care if they tear you down
I have a ghostly picture
a beautiful agent
looking down from the roof
deck like a sailor's widow
with a grandeur
no one will remember

Celebrity Song

It's that tricky time of year,
when greasy, worthless hacks
sweep the awards shows
and I try to ride my malice
into spring, juiced on whatever's
in season, then wind up
hospitalized for exhaustion.

Some gigs the costume
doesn't fit—I blame
the camera and its blasted
fifteen pounds, blame the boy
director climbing daddy's chair.

Sometimes an old bear
needs the electric
collar to make her dance.

You want to be famous?

Marry and divorce.
Keep a doctor close. Take
what makes you better,
like a baseball player.

Love the moment
when you step down
from the trailer, and
fifteen hours later when
you curl up in tears.
Love the lines
before you speak,

the whole scene playing
to your perfect side. Smile
and smile and be
a villain. Hate the taut
bitch nipping in her
four-inch heels.

If TV calls, say yes.
Throw your hair
when the asshole
makes a pass. Lean
in and tell the one
about your own wardrobe
malfunction. Tell the
one about your little
brother's accident. Tell
the one about the snow.

Photoshop

There is a secret
orchid to make you
fall in love with the first
flawed face you see.

I came back from the East

I came back from the East
via the terrible Ohio

highway and moved in with Kenny who
got up with the sun on Saturdays

brewed a pot of teeth-knocking coffee
and drove off to garage sales

where he tried to pick up women
his theory was that early in the morning

you could see them in their natural state
their hair in quick ponytails

legs in frayed orange shorts once
he came home with a turntable some

Tony Bennett records a partial suit of armor
and a kindergarten teacher named Sarah

I was reading want ads at Kenny's ten-dollar
kitchen table they reminded me of poems

no one who amounted to anything
ever looked at them

Sarah had a silver stud in her nose and
I wondered if it scared the kids

I made omelets with garlic and parsley
Kenny propped his armor on an old mop handle

and clanged a wooden spoon
on the chestpiece like a dinner gong

Sarah laughed a cloud of smoke
when she saw Kenny's Louis Prima

records and taxidermied armadillo
and the three turntables

already stacked up on his dresser
I think he was worried about the future

Retrospective

Turn the skate park on its side
and it looks like a Richard Serra
exhibition, studded art lovers high
on particle and wave. For the MoMA
show I came north from Philly
on the Chinatown bus. The crowds
surveyed the lead props, the rubber
belts drooping from walls, then awed
at ten thousand tons of tortuous
steel—a future city one woman
sprinted through in pink sneakers,
her own attempt at art I guess.

Outside the sky was dull as news-
print rolling off a giant press.

Memorize the starry-

memorize the starry-
eyed the Dadaist
sculpture of collapsing
barns scrutinize the purple circuitry
of your own translucent wrist
with the same attention you
give to mapping
Nurse Anne's thighs

our lives are rising
streaming toward the sun

the flowerbeds stink of gunpowder

the jagged cars
abandoned by the curb
look like they've been sitting there
a thousand years

a toast to Anne
to the ones who watch
our bodies disappear

Summer Drowning

A gang of crows
eyed the woman's body,
her hair a muddy delta
on the riverbank.

A skinny warrior
awaiting her funeral pyre?

The local anchor
didn't think so. He
made sure we knew
she was a junkie.

Paramedics came reeking
of French fries and cigarettes
and loaded her on a gurney.

The crows thought that was funny.

A Comedy

Nurse Anne dragged me out for one
last drink, the month before
her wedding. She wondered what it meant
to be a *wife*—a word

that made me flinch so violently
I almost spilled my gin. *Jealousy is never*
charming, Nurse Anne said, licking
salt from her margarita. She said she missed

smoking, *And trying everything once.*
I wondered how long we would perpetuate
this ruthless fantasy. Then she was gone,
a napkin shredded beside her empty glass.

I stayed in the city, buying drinks
for the unemployed. She moved
her lawyer to the broad lawns
of Oak Park. Get it?

I left the comfort of the sea

I left the comfort of the sea
for the Inland Empire for Peter

Pan and Asperger's and drought
for the doubt of a minor painter

I refuse to sleep until I get
the hang of time of television's

wide hours and half-hours
its Martin and Charlie Sheens

scrims and screens through which
we see ourselves Lost Boys

staggering across the wall
in that old parable

sleep is too slow a verb
for this new world

Tonight I am kicking down the doors

tonight I am kicking down the doors
three black rats hunch on their splayed pink feet

in the kitchen and bicker over a ripped-up
bag of Ruffles there's nothing left

on the walls except a painting of two kids
staring out across a lake at the word NIXON

perched in stenciled letters on the water
I don't envy painters anymore

they have to give everything away
they all use text in their work nowadays

these painters should hire me to tell them
which words are good which ones stick

in the throat like cancer pills
Nixon is a good-sounding word

blister and eclipse and possum
are all good and doorframe

what I can never get behind
is an ugly word for a pretty thing

bucolic is such a word shrike is such a word
Uranus is such a word as is panties

possum is a pretty word for an ugly thing
possums play dead until the dog is gone

haven't we all done that a time or two
under our black hedges

my old friend Bill Bennett used to charge out drunk
whenever he saw a possum and give it a good kick

before it could scuttle under the neighbor's fence
when he really got his foot into one

it would curl its evil eraser nose
under its body and lie there playing dead but Bill

was no dumb predator he would get a running start
and give it another blistering kick or fall down

trying and when he caught one just right he could
get some serious air under a possum once he jacked one clear

over the eight-foot fence when Bill got stoned
he would aim the speakers out the window

and dance in the grass like a wild horse
last I heard he'd become a Scientologist

and believed an alien dictator named Xenu
froze millions of his rebellious subjects

and shipped them to earth in cargo planes
stacked the planes around volcanoes

and set off nuclear explosions in all the craters
God how beautiful that must have been

seventy-five billion years later here I am
trying to run off these three imperturbable rats

who keep circling back circling back
until I summon the spirit of Bill Bennett

and BOOM BOOM BOOM kick them all out the door
into the front yard and they go running

down the slope dive into the creek and paddle
away with their noses stuck above the water

fuck all the experiments
fuck Bill Bennett and his stoned exuberance

when I smoked pot all I did was watch *Raising Arizona*
fifty times now I'm in this empty room listening

to the rats moving in the sewer pipe
making their way back towards the house

like buried memories digging for the surface
for twenty years you in the doorframe

shaking your head at the stupid boys
under the long straight hair you wore

then and Bill Bennett's beautiful crazed
face and a possum ringed with porchlight

flying in its destined arc and landing in the darkness
like an alien spacecraft

Acknowledgments

Thanks to the editors of the following journals in which some of these poems first appeared:

AGNI online: "Solomon's Wisdom" and "Retrospective"
American Poetry Journal: "Night Birds"
Black Warrior Review online: "Extremist Sonnet" and "I left the comfort of the sea"
Burnside Review: "Odds"
Columbia Poetry Review: "The geese had lost their minds"
Everyday Genius: "Tonight I am kicking down the doors"
Drunken Boat: "Tailed by swirling buzzards I descended"
FIELD: "First a forest burned" and "Slow and stately survives"
Gulf Coast: "A woman in Dior"
New Ohio Review: "I came back from the East"
Poetry Northwest: "Occupy" and "I want the Internet to stop"
Sixth Finch: "I step away from the oil fires"
Sonora Review: "Social Media"
Southern Indiana Review: "Those Who Favor Fire" and "Each year gave us portals"
Third Coast: "A blade of geese"
Willow Springs: "More and more"

"I saw you crossing Delaware" was printed as a broadside by Blue Satellite Press.

Thank you to David Young, David Walker, Marco Wilkinson, Steve Farkas, and everyone at Oberlin College Press for their incredible support and dedication.

Thank you Robin Behn, Bruce Smith, Tim Berg, Sean Lovelace, Tim Earley, Pete Christman, and Martha Christman.

Thanks Mom, Dad, Sophia, and Juliet for many years of love and encouragement.

To Jill, Ella, and Henry: thank you for this lucky life.

The FIELD Poetry Series

1993   Dennis Schmitz, *About Night: Selected and New Poems*
Marianne Boruch, *Moss Burning*

1994   Russell Edson, *The Tunnel: Selected Poems*

1996   Killarney Clary, *By Common Salt*

1997   Marianne Boruch, *A Stick That Breaks and Breaks*

1998   Jon Loomis, *Vanitas Motel*
Franz Wright, *Ill Lit: Selected & New Poems*

1999   Marcia Southwick, *A Saturday Night at the Flying Dog and Other Poems*

2000   Timothy Kelly, *Stronger*

2001   Ralph Burns, *Ghost Notes*
Jon Loomis, *The Pleasure Principle*

2002   Angie Estes, *Voice-Over*
Tom Andrews, *Random Symmetries: The Collected Poems of Tom Andrews*

2003   Carol Moldaw, *The Lightning Field*

2004   Marianne Boruch, *Poems: New & Selected*
Jonah Winter, *Amnesia*

2005   Angie Estes, *Chez Nous*
Beckian Fritz Goldberg, *Lie Awake Lake*

2006   Jean Gallagher, *Stubborn*

2007   Mary Cornish, *Red Studio*

2008   J. W. Marshall, *Meaning a Cloud*
Timothy Kelly, *The Extremities*

2009   Dennis Hinrichsen, *Kurosawa's Dog*
Angie Estes, *Tryst*

2010   Amy Newlove Schroeder, *The Sleep Hotel*

2011   Timothy O'Keefe, *The Goodbye Town*

2012   Jean Gallagher, *Start*
Mark Neely, *Beasts of the Hill*

2013   Mary Ann Samyn, *My Life in Heaven*
Beckian Fritz Goldberg, *Egypt from Space*
Angie Estes, *Enchantée*

2014   Bern Mulvey, *Deep Snow Country*
Dennis Schmitz, *Animism*

2015   Carol Potter, *Some Slow Bees*
Mark Neely, *Dirty Bomb*

78731 U. S. A. Telephone: (512) 451-4464.
Facsimile: (512) 451-4464.

United Kingdom and Europe: (VAT
is added where applicable.) International
Book Distributors, Ltd., Campus 400,
Maylands Avenue, Hemel Hempstead HP2
7EZ, England. Telephone: 0442
881900/Telex: 82445. Facsimile: 0442
882099. Internet:
536-2875@MCIMAIL.COM

**Australia, New Zealand, South
Pacific, Africa, Middle East, China
(PRC), Southeast Asia, and India:**
The University of Chicago Press,
International Sales Manager, 5801 South
Ellis Avenue, Chicago, Illinois 60637
U.S.A. Telephone: (312)702 7706.
Facsimile: (312)702-9756.
Internet: dblobaum@press.uchicago.edu

Japan: Libraries and individuals should
place their orders with local booksellers.
Booksellers should place orders with our
agent: United Publishers Services, Ltd.,
Kenkyu-sha Building, 9 Kanda Surugadai
2-chome, Chiyoda-ku, Tokyo, Japan.
Telephone: (03)3291-4541. Facsimile:
(03)3293-8610. Telex: J33331 (answerback
UPSTOKYO). Cable: UNITEDBOOKS
TOKYO.

**Korea, Hong Kong, and Taiwan,
R.O.C.:** The America University Press
Group, 3-21-18-206 Higashi-Shinagawa,
Shinagawa-ku, Tokyo 140, Japan.
Telephone: (03)3450-2857. Facsimile:
(03)3472-9706.

CSLI Titles Distributed by CSLI Publications

*Hausar Yau Da Kullum: Intermediate and
Advanced Lessons in Hausa Language
and Culture.* Leben, Zaria, Maikafi,
and Yalwa. 0-937073-68-7 (paper)

Hausar Yau Da Kullum Workbook.
Leben, Zaria, Maikafi, and Yalwa.
0-93703-69-5 (paper)

Ordering Titles Distributed by CSLI

Titles distributed by CSLI may be ordered
directly from CSLI Publications, Ventura
Hall, Stanford, CA 94305-4115. Orders
can also be placed by FAX (415)723-0758
or e-mail (pubs@csli.stanford.edu).

All orders must be prepaid by check or
Visa or MasterCard (include card name,
number, and expiration date). California
residents add 8.25% sales tax. For
shipping and handling, add $2.50 for first
book and $0.75 for each additional book;
$1.75 for first report and $0.25 for each
additional report.

For overseas shipping, add $4.50 for first
book and $2.25 for each additional book;
$2.25 for first report and $0.75 for each
additional report. All payments must be
made in U.S. currency.

CSLI Publications on the World-Wide Web

Please visit CSLI Publications'
World-Wide Web page at:
http://csli-www.stanford.edu/publications/
for a complete and updated list of
publications.

Internet Gopher Access: University of
Chicago Press catalogs can be searched
on-line by connecting to the University of
Chicago Press gopher:

press-gopher.uchicago.edu

The Proceedings of the Thirteenth West
Coast Conference on Formal
Linguistics (WCCFL 13). Aranovich,
Byrne, Preuss, Senturia (Eds.).
1-881526-76-3 (paper),

The Proceedings of the Fourteenth West
Coast Conference on Formal
Linguistics (WCCFL 14). Camacho,
Choueri, & Watanabe (Eds.).
1-57586-042-2 (paper), 1-57586-043-0

European Review of Philosophy:
Philosophy of Mind. Soldati (Ed.).
1-881526-38-0 (paper), 1-881526-53-4

Experiencer Subjects in South Asian
Languages. Verma and Mohanan
(Eds.). 0-937073-60-1 (paper),
0-937073-61-X

Grammatical Relations: A
Cross-Theoretical Perspective.
Dziwirek, Farrell, Bikandi (Eds.).
0-937073-63-6 (paper), 0-937073-62-8

Grammatical Relations: Theoretical
Approaches to Empirical Questions.
Burgess, Dziwirek, Gerdts, (Eds.).
1-57586-002-3 (paper), 1-57586-003-1

Theoretical Issues in Korean Linguistics.
Kim-Renaud (Ed.). 1-881526-51-8
(paper), 1-881526-52-6

Agreement in Natural Language:
Approaches, Theories, Descriptions.
Barlow and Ferguson (Eds.).
0-937073-02-4

Papers from the Second International
Workshop on Japanese Syntax. Poser
(Ed.). 0-937073-38-5 (paper),
0-937073-39-3

Conceptual Structure, Discourse and
Language. Goldberg, (Ed.).
1-57586-040-6 (paper), 1-57586-041-4

Sociolinguistic Variation. Arnold et al.
(Eds.). 1-57586-038-4 (paper),
1-57586-039-2

Ordering Titles from Cambridge University Press

Titles distributed by Cambridge
University Press may be ordered directly
from the distributor at 110 Midland
Avenue, Port Chester, NY 10573-4930
(USA), or by phone: 914-937-9600,
1-800-872-7423 (US and Canada),
95-800-010-0200 (Mexico). You may also
order by fax at 914-937-4712.

Overseas Orders

Cambridge University Press has offices
worldwide which serve the international
community.

Australia: Cambridge University Press,
120 Stamford Road, Oakleigh, Victoria
31266, Australia. phone: (613) 563-1517.
fax: 613 563 1517.

**UK, Europe, Asia, Africa, South
America:** Cambridge University Press,
Publishing Division, The Edinburgh
Building, Shaftesbury Road, Cambridge
CB2 2RU, UK.

Inquiries: (phone) 44 1223 312393
(fax) 44 1223 315052

Orders: (phone) 44 1223 325970
(fax) 44 1223 325959

CSLI Titles Distributed by The University of Chicago Press

The Phonology-Syntax Connection.
Inkelas and Zec. 0-226-38100-5
(paper), 0-226-38101-3

On What We Know We Don't Know.
Bromberger. 0-226-07540-0 (paper),
0-226-07539-7

Arenas of Language Use. Clark.
0-226-10782-5 (paper), 0-226-10781-7

Head-Driven Phrase Structure Grammar.
Pollard and Sag. 0-226-67447-9 (paper)

Titles distributed by The University of
Chicago Press may be ordered directly
from UCP. Phone 1-800-621-2736. Fax
(800) 621-8471.

Titles distributed by The University of
Chicago Press may be ordered directly
from UCP. Phone 1-800-621-2736. Fax
(800) 621-8471.

Overseas Orders

The University of Chicago Press has
offices worldwide which serve the
international community.

**Mexico, Central America, South
America, and the Caribbean
(including Puerto Rico):** EDIREP,
5500 Ridge Oak Drive, Austin, Texas

On the Placement and Morphology of Clitics. Halpern. 1-881526-60-7 (paper), 1-881526-61-5

The Structure of Complex Predicates in Urdu. Butt. 1-881526-59-3 (paper), 1-881562-58-5

Configuring Topic and Focus in Russia. King. 1-881526-63-1 (paper), 1-881562-62-3

The Semantic Basis of Argument Structure. Wechsler. 1-881526-68-2 (paper), 1-881562-69-0

Stricture in Feature Geometry. Padgett. 1-881526-66-6 (paper), 1-881562-67-4

Possessive Descriptions. Barker. 1-881526-72-0 (paper), 1-881562-73-9

Studies in Logic, Language and Information

Logic Colloquium '92. Csirmaz, Gabbay, and de Rijke (Eds.). 1-881526-98-4 (paper), 1-881526-97-6

Meaning and Partiality. Muskens. 1-881526-79-8 (paper), 1-881526-80-1

Logic and Visual Information. Hammer. 1-881526-99-2 (paper), 1-881526-87-9

Partiality, Modality and Nonmonotonicity. Doherty. 1-57586 030 0 (paper), 1-57586-031-7

Basic Model Theory. Doets. 1-57586-048-1 (paper), 1-57586-049-X

Studies in Japanese Linguistics

The Syntax of Subjects. Tateishi. 1-881526-45-3 (paper), 1-881526-46-1

Theory of Projection in Syntax. Fukui. 1-881526-34-8 (paper), 1-881526-35-6

A Study of Japanese Clause Linkage: The Connective TE in Japanese. Hasegawa. 1-57586-026-0 (paper), 1-57586-027-9

Other CSLI Titles Distributed by Cambridge University Press

The Proceedings of the Twenty-Fourth Annual Child Language Research Forum. Clark (Ed.). 1-881526-05-4 (paper), 1-881526-04-6

The Proceedings of the Twenty-Fifth Annual Child Language Research Forum. Clark (Ed.). 1-881526-31-3 (paper), 1-881526-33-X

The Proceedings of the Twenty-Sixth Annual Child Language Research Forum. Clark (Ed.). 1-881526-31-3 (paper), 1-881526-33-X

Japanese/Korean Linguistics. Hoji (Ed.). 0-937073-57-1 (paper), 0-937073-56-3

Japanese/Korean Linguistics, Vol. 2. Clancy (Ed.). 1-881526-13-5 (paper), 1-881526-14-3

Japanese/Korean Linguistics, Vol. 3. Choi (Ed.). 1-881526-21-6 (paper), 1-881526-22-4

Japanese/Korean Linguistics, Vol. 4. Akatsuka (Ed.). 1-881526-64-X (paper), 1-881526-65-8

Japanese/Korean Linguistics, Vol. 5. Akatasuka, Iwasaki, & Strauss (Eds.). 1-57586-044-9 (paper), 1-57586-045-7

The Proceedings of the Fourth West Coast Conference on Formal Linguistics (WCCFL 4). 0-937073-43-1 (paper)

The Proceedings of the Fifth West Coast Conference on Formal Linguistics (WCCFL 5). 0-937073-42-3 (paper)

The Proceedings of the Sixth West Coast Conference on Formal Linguistics (WCCFL 6). 0-937073-31-8 (paper)

The Proceedings of the Seventh West Coast Conference on Formal Linguistics (WCCFL 7). 0-937073-40-7 (paper)

The Proceedings of the Eighth West Coast Conference on Formal Linguistics (WCCFL 8). 0-937073-45-8 (paper)

The Proceedings of the Ninth West Coast Conference on Formal Linguistics (WCCFL 9). 0-937073-64-4 (paper)

The Proceedings of the Tenth West Coast Conference on Formal Linguistics (WCCFL 10). 0-937073-79-2 (paper)

The Proceedings of the Eleventh West Coast Conference on Formal Linguistics (WCCFL 11). Mead (Ed.). 1-881526-12-7 (paper),

The Proceedings of the Twelfth West Coast Conference on Formal Linguistics (WCCFL 12). Duncan, Farkas, Spaelti (Eds.). 1-881526-33-X (paper),

Verbmobil: A Translation System for Face-to-Face Dialog. Kay, Gawron, and Norvig. No. 33. 0-937073-95-4 (paper), 0-937073-96-2

The Language of First-Order Logic (including the Windows program, Tarski's World 4.0). Barwise and Etchemendy, 3rd edition. No. 34. 0-937073-90-3 (paper)

Turing's World. Barwise and Etchemendy. No. 35. 1-881526-10-0 (paper)

The Syntax of Anaphoric Binding. Dalrymple. No. 36. 1-881526-06-2 (paper), 1-881526-07-0

Situation Theory and Its Applications, Vol. 3. Aczel, Israel, Katagiri, and Peters (Eds.). No. 37. 1-881526-08-9 (paper), 1-881526-09-7

Theoretical Aspects of Bantu Grammar. Mchombo (Ed.). No. 38. 0-937073-72-5 (paper), 0-937073-73-3

Logic and Representation. Moore. No. 39. 1-881526-15-1 (paper), 1-881526-16-X

Language and Learning for Robots. Crangle and Suppes. No. 41. 1-881526-19-4 (paper), 1-881526-20-8

Hyperproof. Barwise and Etchemendy. No. 42. 1-881526-11-9 (paper)

Mathematics of Modality. Goldblatt. No. 43. 1-881526-23-2 (paper), 1-881526-24-0

Feature Logics, Infinitary Descriptions, and Grammar. Keller. No. 44. 1-881526-25-9 (paper), 1-881526-26-7

Tarski's World: Windows Version 4.0. Barwise and Etchemendy. No. 45. 1-881526-28-3 (paper)

German in Head-Driven Phrase Structure Grammar. Pollard, Nerbonne, and Netter. No. 46. 1-881526-29-1 (paper), 1-881526-30-5

Formal Issues in Lexical-Functional Grammar. Dalrymple and Zaenen. No. 47. 1-881526-36-4 (paper), 1-881526-37-2

Dynamics, Polarity, and Quantification. Kanazawa and Piñón. No. 48. 1-881526-41-0 (paper), 1-881526-42-9

Defending AI Research: A Collection of Essays and Reviews. McCarthy. No. 49. 1-57586-018-X (paper), 1-57586-019-8

Theoretical Perspectives on Word Order in South Asian Languages. Butt, King, and Ramchand. No. 50. 1-881526-49-6 (paper), 1-881526-50-X

Perspectives in Phonology. Cole and Kisseberth. No. 51. 1-881526-54-2 (paper), 1-881526-55-0

Linguistics and Computation. Cole, Green, and Morgan. No. 52. 1-881526-81-X (paper), 1-881526-82-8

Modal Logic and Process Algebra: A Bisimulation Approach. Ponse, de Rijke, and Venema. No. 53. 1-881526-96-8 (paper), 1-881526-95-X

Quantifiers, Logic, and Language. van der Does and van Eijck. No. 54. 1-57586-000-7 (paper), 1-57586-001-5

Semantic Ambiguity and Underspecification. van Deemter and Peters. No. 55. 1-57586-028-7 (paper), 1-57586-029-5

Necessity or Contingency. Vuillemin. No. 56. 1-881526-85-2 (paper), 1-881526-86-0

Quantifiers, Deduction, and Context. Kanazawa, Piñón, & de Swart. No. 57. 1-57586-005-8 (paper), 1-57586-004-X

Logic, Language and Computation. Seligman & Westerståhl. No. 58. 1-881526-89-5 (paper), 1-881526-90-9

Selected Papers on Computer Science. Knuth. No. 59. 1-881526-917 (paper), 1-881526-925

Vicious Circles. Barwise & Moss. No. 60. 1-57586-008-2 (paper), 1-57586-009-0

Approaching Second. Halpern & Zwicky. No. 61. 1-57586-014-7 (paper), 1-57586-015-5

The Role of Argument Structure in Grammar. Alsina. No. 62. 1-57586-034-1 (paper), 1-57586-035-X

Dissertations in Linguistics Series

Phrase Structure and Grammatical Relations in Tagalog. Kroeger. 0-937073-86-5 (paper), 0-937073-87-3

Theoretical Aspects of Kashaya Phonology and Morphology. Buckley. 1-881526-02-X (paper), 1-881526-03-8

Argument Structure in Hindi. Mohanan. 1-881526-43-7 (paper), 1-881526-44-5

CSLI Publications

CSLI Publications are distributed world-wide by Cambridge University Press unless otherwise noted.

Lecture Notes

A Manual of Intensional Logic. van Benthem, 2nd edition. No. 1. 0-937073-29-6 (paper), 0-937073-30-X

Lectures on Contemporary Syntactic Theories. Sells. No. 3. 0-937073-14-8 (paper), 0-937073-13-X

The Semantics of Destructive Lisp. Mason. No. 5. 0-937073-06-7 (paper), 0 937073 05-9

An Essay on Facts. Olson. No. 6. 0-937073-08-3 (paper), 0-937073-05-9

Logics of Time and Computation. Goldblatt, 2nd edition. No. 7. 0-937073-94-6 (paper), 0-937073-93-8

Word Order and Constituent Structure in German. Uszkoreit. No. 8. 0-937073-10-5 (paper), 0-937073-09-1

Color and Color Perception: A Study in Anthropocentric Realism. Hilbert. No. 9. 0-937073-16-4 (paper), 0-937073-15-6

Prolog and Natural-Language Analysis. Pereira and Shieber. No. 10. 0-937073-18-0 (paper), 0-937073-17-2

Working Papers in Grammatical Theory and Discourse Structure: Interactions of Morphology, Syntax, and Discourse. Iida, Wechsler, and Zec (Eds.). No. 11. 0-937073-04-0 (paper), 0-937073-25-3

Natural Language Processing in the 1980s: A Bibliography. Gazdar, Franz, Osborne, and Evans. No. 12. 0-937073-28-8 (paper), 0-937073-26-1

Information-Based Syntax and Semantics. Pollard and Sag. No. 13. 0-937073-24-5 (paper), 0-937073-23-7

Non-Well-Founded Sets. Aczel. No. 14. 0-937073-22-9 (paper), 0-937073-21-0

Partiality, Truth and Persistence. Langholm. No. 15. 0-937073-34-2 (paper), 0-937073-35-0

Attribute-Value Logic and the Theory of Grammar. Johnson. No. 16. 0-937073-36-9 (paper), 0-937073-37-7

The Situation in Logic. Barwise. No. 17. 0-937073-32-6 (paper), 0-937073-33-4

The Linguistics of Punctuation. Nunberg. No. 18. 0-937073-46-6 (paper), 0-937073-47-4

Anaphora and Quantification in Situation Semantics. Gawron and Peters. No. 19. 0-937073-48-4 (paper), 0-937073-49-0

Propositional Attitudes: The Role of Content in Logic, Language, and Mind. Anderson and Owens. No. 20. 0-937073-50-4 (paper), 0-937073-51-2

Literature and Cognition. Hobbs. No. 21. 0-937073-52-0 (paper), 0-937073-53-9

Situation Theory and Its Applications, Vol. 1. Cooper, Mukai, and Perry (Eds.). No. 22. 0-937073-54-7 (paper), 0-937073-55-5

The Language of First-Order Logic (including the Macintosh program, Tarski's World 4.0). Barwise and Etchemendy, 3rd Edition. No. 23. 0-937073-99-7 (paper)

Lexical Matters. Sag and Szabolcsi (Eds.). No. 24. 0-937073-66-0 (paper), 0-937073-65-2

Tarski's World: Macintosh Version 4.0. Barwise and Etchemendy. No. 25. 1-881526-27-5 (paper)

Situation Theory and Its Applications, Vol. 2. Barwise, Gawron, Plotkin, and Tutiya (Eds.). No. 26. 0-937073-70-9 (paper), 0-937073-71-7

Literate Programming. Knuth. No. 27. 0-937073-80-6 (paper), 0-937073-81-4

Normalization, Cut-Elimination and the Theory of Proofs. Ungar. No. 28. 0-937073-82-2 (paper), 0-937073-83-0

Lectures on Linear Logic. Troelstra. No. 29. 0-937073-77-6 (paper), 0-937073-78-4

A Short Introduction to Modal Logic. Mints. No. 30. 0-937073-75-X (paper), 0-937073-76-8

Linguistic Individuals. Ojeda. No. 31. 0-937073-84-9 (paper), 0-937073-85-7

Computational Models of American Speech. Withgott and Chen. No. 32. 0-937073-98-9 (paper), 0-937073-97-0

For Jill

The FIELD Poetry Series, vol. 35
Oberlin College Press, 50 N. Professor Street, Oberlin, OH 44074
www.oberlin.edu/ocpress

Book design: Steve Farkas
Cover image: Harold E. Edgerton, "Bullet Through Apple" (1964).
Photograph © 2010 MIT. Courtesy of MIT Museum.

Library of Congress Cataloging-in-Publication Data

Neely, Mark, 1971-
[Poems. Selections]
Dirty bomb / Mark Neely.
    pages ; cm. — (Field poetry series ; vol. 35)
    ISBN 978-0-932440-49-5 (softcover : acid-free paper) —
    ISBN 0-932440-49-5 (softcover : acid-free paper)
    I. Title.
    PS3614.E36A6 2015
    811'.6—dc23
                                    2014038530

DIRTY BOMB

Mark Neely

Oberlin College Press
Oberlin, Ohio

DIRTY BOMB

Contents

Far thunder at dead of night, I wake to it, a low rumble along the horizon, the air crumpling. I imagine what it must be like out there, out beyond the land, where the humped sea hugely heaves, black as oilskin under a bulging clay-dark sky; I imagine it, and I am there.

—John Banville

To bend nature, as a wand . . .

—Sir Francis Bacon

Accommodo

Ice pigeon, the slender neck of isosceles cloud,
      by noon we are passengers in the occluded

front, fly screens opened to their individual will,
      the new cold all twisting and writhing,

goldenrod in their gifted seizures, one thing
      a looking glass into its other, no rules

for haunting, the sumac wearing its inverted cones
      like choral music —flickers, robins, finches

I am afraid of stars

Acer

Maple with the skulls of young birds
     will cost you everything—

I pour you a glass of milk, warm and salty
     as the new grave of great flies, the air

a Dead Sea of leaf and rain, I am with knots
     in my hair cleaning all dust

all driving wind, feather-footing
     the weather-change, please come for me

should I go out beyond the land

Aperio

Hamstrung by their close resemblance to ghosts,
      early apples, the Paula Reds, sweet enough

to make a grave unsteady—whomever saved me
      never looked up, but held awfully cold doves

in green loops of field air, so much math
      in early trees, mom and dad

each a slice of knot unsolved, their bodies healed
      and flown, enough room to unravel

eleven kinds of crossings

Appono

Cardinal left early to build itself air
        copper today in the humid fibers

of unsourced salt he picks from the brook-bed
        of lightweight earth, tintypes of goldfinch

and the name of someone who cannot stop
        slowing the less carnivorous wind—

My boy fills himself with fossil plants
        and soil and looks not back, but at water

falling on the pewter wires in the wooded sun

Appareo

In the shivering wet, rain a place of light
      ahead of us, its monologue a weakness

on my part because I'll listen, I'll monitor
      the tendons of lightning, the living shipwrecks

of oak, I'll spend all night getting it wrong,
      the cheap wind no one wanted,

cylinders of geese in their ground-glowing flesh,
      the lacquer of any summer ghost

gone soft into the delicate fronds of plant

Accipio

The land leans to lesser periwinkle
        in the chaos of sun, swarming,

green-slammed into rain, I
        am there as swamp silkweed, larger

bindweed, chicory like a spirit crawling
        the roots, I

am calm there taking the ground's
        temperature each time

its birth settles down

Altus

Soul—chokecherry winter-cooked
     by the salty balance, cardinal with a halt

in the water then storms of it, so much spun glass
     coming down, the polite distance of you

whinnying, like gray stone whinnying,
     not a noise from a horse named Caesar,

but the center of the coded horizon, such soft
     weight of compost left—

I am hardly here at all

Articulus

Forgiveness, I am quiet under the damned
        eyes of birds, like an old man killing things

aglow, muttering something shut tight
        in wood-wild sound, it's not nightfall

I am seeing, the slow dive of horizon weaned
        sheepishly from day, light in its

fainthearted sap and the staggering
        white circle so convincing

it could be breath

Astrum

The muscle-bound assassin
　　　that is sun—understand

she is leaving us—I know it takes a moment,
　　　east of the Rockies Dunlin sandpipers

hunch un-patterned, tide-halted
　　　with the varnished sand

and krill, and when moon spills
　　　its thorns, the soul

has to get away hard

Audax

Light of the kinglet—remind us
    we are burning too

Have I already said this?
    Have I

in freshwater and slack wonder
    been breathing

the wind all along?
    the sky is buttered

then pulses blue, look—falling rain

Aureus

Forest and the dove grow huge,
        throw their bodies to silt soil

inside the slighter shock of August,
        I should remember a ghost has a habit

of speech, I should be that golden, half-starved
        sound, hair below my waist

taking note of plover drift, field back toward the first
        floating tantrum of the feathery

world, just a layer of far love

Bellum

The sea is loaded, is plover
      having heard the land looks too hot

that slurred whistle a damp stagger
      in fog—what shall be,

what shall be done? At the petting zoo
      my boy waited, but the peacock

wouldn't cry, now both of us in this cold
      church of ocean

making that loud plumage scream

Brevitas

Without me, you are getting ready—
    monarchs in a stretch of milkweed

still thinking they're everything—jewelweed,
    old-field toadflax, barely rain-splashed

for what might hold the earth to earth,
    bite marks on groundhogs, folded birds

that once traveled on the slapped back of ghosts—
    you're painting in bed again

before being able to float away

Cautela

For all we know
      we haven't been terrible, but nesting

fluent in quiver, but you are barefoot in the language
      of the lamb milk clouds,

aortic light real as any one heart, the planet itself
      resting on the cool half-halted riot of monarchs,

I mean all of it—the north-facing century
      even if we don't keep seated

in rolling chant in hemlock tangles

Cohors

Morning, milk snake, wind, it softened me—
    white hydrangeas anointed

as ice caps, you left your little blue bed as leaves
    foiled, pollen on thick ropes of pollen, you

and the neighbor's kid went to collect
    rainwater—let us have your art!—

we're out of shade, all-but-invisible here
    with our tongues in our mouths   believe me

this is why I never learned to crave myself

Defluo

I believed badly in the un-mothered sun
     raw as deadened eggs,

the smell of the dark too weak
     in its blue veins, only the steaming

stone, the high tragedy of hawks,
     the long answers so bored

with us they come now as new swallows
     feeding their own

like hot gold smoke in the local pond

Dirunitas

I have to lie a little about the freshwater here,
    shock the self-sown firs

into final stars—anything small could choose me
    because we must go away raw

because only animals interrupt the shedding
    tiers of chestnuts curled up

in the throes of older chestnuts, even the explicit
    order of soil is a completely strange story

deep, hot and acting like dust

Divinus

So alone I've become a hexagon, one of the living
        roots, but you—little witness

you—with your musk turtles, scraps of duckweed
        in your flaxen hair, your body reading

its own red clover, a gland of cloud
        in trouble, the startling fact of nectar,

you and the pond-matter starting all over for what
        I assume is love that stepped forward

in the rained-on grace between lives

Donec

Who will venerate the saints coming back salt,
    all salt, hydrangea and snail?

In the other room the seawalls drip
    their mewling noise, last March

when you touched the heavyweight seal
    everything in you became boy,

and when you are no longer
    the cranial nerves of water

I will smell you, out beyond the land

Eruo

Harm and wild, we picked fennel and bunching alliums,
    wonder coming in with her lemony hips—

I licked my hand to sow my boy's bed hair,
    basil, then nothing but acoustics blowing loose

matter around the dirt, the living earth of Saturday
    and casts from worms like old bourbon

and the manic slowness of cooked rain—
    Come imagine we are not seeing

cells all trying to shape equal spheres

Expostulo

Later, ocean is drawn to its margins
    the water's green wax left ungnawed,

no bluefish bulky in the sediment,
    you ask the humblest parasite to cling

to the odd punk of driftwood, no love for the gods
    who have gone under, no iron birds melted down,

you give me your stuffed seal pup to wash
    if only to launder the delicate

grown thick, the breathy distress of now

Extorqueo

Roseroot, sedum in depressions of rock ledges
     dislocated in soft earth falling apart

in tropical-force rain, the type of jury
     any storm can be, the swollen line

of forecast like red yarn on a bloated doll
     —and if we are result not reason?—

my little boy wincing to sleep, his clavicle
     a broken copy of the air,

the love-waste of wind

Fabula

Parent, daughter, oil, shale—
        tomato vines separated in watermark

shine, those who have attended to birds
        and come home to hear them

O' upwelling—I am completely healed
        of waiting, sorrel grows in acid soil,

the flowers yellow and green, the breathing
        are only species of those without breath,

drafts of yellow thistle staring back uphill

Femina

Call this unfolding an oscillation
     of sea, blued-eyed and deaf to its own

astonishing, old sand giving no answer
     like the loggerheaded duck, poor diver

incapable of true flight, part of lonely
     is being struck by feathers,

I must say a few words
     to God now flaring such sunset

all of my hair is cardinals

Filius

The sun a postcard from every planted moment,
       running, rapid heart, the active effort

of daisies, I first thought the shadow was well
       within the willow-herb, nothing for it

to chew but ground, today every rock you chucked
       in ocean came back as floating clay,

I read you a poem about alligators and ended
       up believing in good deaths,

sorry my boy, even I will taste the final rust

Forte

I want to tell you a story of waterleaf
   whose stamens extend

beyond the flowers, but I am preserved
   with breath—Part of this rain

is not important within its warp,
      so instead of calling it a story

I'll tell you it's spillway, I'll draw it
      on your other shoulder,

the one that didn't break

Gravitas

Our garden is pacemaker more than art—
      water for the hand-marbled boy

polite with quail eggs, even here
      the horses are undressed

because you need to think of them
      as nude for rain,

rock-pigeons green and go small into
      the weighted wind and I give

you the single transit of my right hand

Humo

I lay your clowns graveside
      in their pulped paper,

the first night I stood canted
      and cried snow,

because movement is recorded
      I poured the wine

twice, moody in the matt blue
      midnight of here,

somewhere a boat, a grand tug

Infinitus

Ocean is a tendency,
       the part of us that turns

unreal with petals the way a horse
       becomes dolphin

when it touches sea, a boy
       crosses a bridge

with a homemade slingshot,
       the world and its linings

with its quiet weaponry

Juvenis

Oaks, little links dropping anchor to the tertiaries
    that travel straight down, sinkers

and rootlets in their water search, my boy damaged
    waving his sling at the wrens,

the worker ants windless on his red shoes,
    I could pass through solid objects

if he needed pine bark, what I believe
    disappears in the unwashed

sweat of our salted burn pile

Lacertosus

Parcels of heat in the hospice of the central orchard,
      blueberries bright by variation, a list

of apples in their southern limit,
      if a plot of ground is beyond the land

it must know how dancers convert
      their movements into a language of wave,

the same math as holograms, dark
      heavy hickories and the interference

patterns of fruited light

Laetans

Bright salts visible and unfinished
      in the exploration of other

oceans, the accidental entanglement
      of the unnamed, its hadal zones

and trenches, I have hopelessly saved gorse
      and goldenrod to throw

at the Atlantic, the tide on its hind legs
      all but panting, the remarkable water

believing beyond its order

Lector

Cranes, nurseries for animals, codes in wetlands,
    the dwindled wanting—I'm afraid

they're calling your name, you're given
    name, earth takes its makeshift parents

into waist-deep water, no one may go near
    the just-hatched chicks who delay

their disappearance, the birds are asleep in miles
    of century and act out in captured light,

vulnerable maybe to the sight of a body

Lentus

Low emission sugar kelp in the offshore
        headlines, marine farms I'll read to him

propped up by pillows, the robotic tether
        of older mothers because I love him,

 his bones flared and bent, his mind in the field
        of healthy flesh of the lower seas,

midnight zone, the abyssal with its tripods
        and black swallowers, the kind

of force it must take to break us

Libero

Variable hawthorn, all that had grown
        apples before rust, lemony scraps

slow to spool and whistling—yes—whistling
        like a stepchild of something far

grayer than sun—when I left home
        I went on like yellow wine

in a tree's world, maybe you heard me,
        glands and bones

and the ninety-nine names for iridescence

Magus

His job, caretaker—his sigh and laugh—the unmoving
   air in trees, days I think he plummeted

to earth just to be lost in marigold, the orthodox
   physics of ocean, each quantum seal pup

a candidate for maintenance, I imagine him after
   I am beyond the land with a thimbleful

of water from purple milkweed, every reason to believe
   we wander and increase, carried regularly

by the nectared act of crossing

Miro

The little ones have laid for the first time
        their best blue eggs

almost aquatic—that we may interfere
        with no direct words

but a list of small plants near the coast
        of old forms, clay soil shrubs

lie dormant in cold silver, then comes March
        in spine and silence—

I kept everything from you

Mortuus

So must the number of wolf eels nest
     in the simmering cold—

Remember that night—the ocean all smoke
     and licorice, compound dawn

as cider and bisque? We might have had parents
     or pale vines, sea dust pushes past

in our sleep, I don't know what to think
     of a mother's bed

moving landward in the waves

Natura

Now that I've seen the seeded beech, its early
    green clothes a flustered bird,

it's true to want winter's two worlds—
    the second state of stigmata's wounds,

fresh tobacco and violets in what would open
    and close on command—

how bedridden the brook will become
    before the whale windows

we call our breaching hearts

Nauta

Ocean buried in the high dark
      sands, ocean with crawl

and shyness out-wept of its riptides,
      its inhalations of osprey,

I cough sunlight and can't be sure
      if I've eaten—crabs, sea lilies

and brittle stars, feather corals tremendous
      in their seamounts—

I reach for what I can't normally reach

Navigo

In the ocean house mirror, horses
        now part of this sea-rain,

osprey no choice but to love
        them as wave—

once, there was far little weight
        to the glass-green clouds,

it wasn't only my body that couldn't
        swim, it meant everything

to say only kelp and love can float

Orbis Terrarum

Trees this autumn will give long answers
    to their last high fever,

the whole underground will turn navy
    and it will be yours

to cut music from the wild hybrid oaks—
    I don't watch you

out of loneliness anymore, I see you have
    another name, a form of skylight

a design for carriers and crows

Pergo

You can do this—the rough walls of wax
      between us, like being asked to dye

each cell of wind to see the moss phlox
      of you and you, so scared to live notched

in that soil, our deaths are only habits
      of decline still spreading the rootstock

of sweet flag, and if the sun is a less modified
      state of soul, here are my twenty-eight acres

to miss you and go on, miss you and go on

Persisto

Water—how we'd run on blue elements
        toward horizon, racing the green-winged teals

until there was nothing more to say
        about sadness, shells snapped

like bass spines, we were whole groups of laws
        in the knots of riptides—

Today, when I shower off the salts turned sweet
        I'll know nothing about this

kneeling has ended in distress

Promissio

What Chestnuts of soul-making, what plantings?—our forest
     shocked by September sharing sunlight

with beryl and smoky quartz, my fear of the butterfly
     in glass a deeper blue than before—soon

I'll know saints by the way each smells of cinnamon,
     when someone dear is about to die

their hair will be cool with lemons, all night
     I'll hold my little boy they way gods do in myths

and the rock pigeon will live his life of forms